VBA for Excel

Made Simple

Computing
Made Simple

Access 2000 Business Edition
STEPHEN
075064611X 1999

ASP NEW!
DEANE
075065869X 2003

Basic Computer Skills
SHERMAN
075064897X 2001

CompuServe 2000
BRINDLEY
0750645245 2000

Designing Internet Home Pages 2ed
HOBBS
0750644761 1999

Dreamweaver
MURPHY
0750654597 2002

ECDL/ICDL 3.0 Office 2000 Revised Edition
BCD Ltd
0750653388 2003

ECDL/ICDL 3.0 Office 97 Edition
BCD Ltd
0750651873 2000

Excel 2002
MORRIS
0750656913 2002

Excel 2000
MORRIS
0750641800 2000

Excel 2000 Business Edition
MORRIS
0750646098 2000

Excel 97 for Windows
MORRIS
0750638028 1997

Excel for Windows 95 (V. 7)
MORRIS
0750628162 1996

Explorer 5
MCBRIDE, P K
0750646276 1999

Flash 5
MCGRATH
0750653612 2001

iMac and iBook
BRINDLEY
075064608X 2000

Internet in Colour 2ed
MCBRIDE, P K
0750645768 1999

Internet for Windows 98
MCBRIDE, P K
0750645636 1999

MS DOS
SINCLAIR
0750620692 1994

Office 2000
MCBRIDE, P K
0750641797 1999

Office XP
MCBRIDE, P K
0750655623 2001

Outlook 2000
MCBRIDE, P K
0750644141 2000

Photoshop
WYNNE-POWELL
075064334X 1999

Pocket PC
PEACOCK
0750649003 2000

Publisher 2000
STEPHEN
0750645970 1999

Project 2000
MURPHY
0750651903 2001

Publisher 97
STEPHEN
0750639431 1998

Sage Accounts 2ed
McBRIDE
075065810X 2002

Searching the Internet
MCBRIDE, P K
0750637943 1998

Windows XP
MCBRIDE, P K
0750656263 2001

Windows ME
MCBRIDE, P K
0750652373 2000

Windows CE
PEACOCK
0750643358 1999

Word 2002
BRINDLEY
0750656905 2002

Word 2000 Business Edition
BRINDLEY
0750646101 2000

Word 97 for Windows
BRINDLEY
075063801X 1997

Works 2000
MCBRIDE, P K
0750649852 2000

XML NEW!
DEANE/HENDERSON
075065998X 2003

WITHDRAWN

ALL YOU NEED TO GET STARTED!

MADE SIMPLE BOOKS

VBA for Excel
Made Simple

Keith Darlington

MADE SIMPLE
BOOKS

AMSTERDAM • BOSTON • HEIDELBERG • LONDON • NEW YORK • OXFORD
PARIS • SAN DIEGO • SAN FRANCISCO • SINGAPORE • SYDNEY • TOKYO

Made Simple
An imprint of Elsevier
Linacre House, Jordan Hill, Oxford OX2 8DP
200 Wheeler Road, Burlington, MA 01803

First published 2004

TRADEMARKS/REGISTERED TRADEMARKS
Computer hardware and software brand names mentioned in this book
are protected by their respective trademarks and are acknowledged.

British Library Cataloguing in Publication Data
A catalogue record for this book is available from the British Library

ISBN 0 7506 6097 X

For information on all Made Simple publications
visit our website at www.madesimple.co.uk

Typeset by Elle and P.K. McBride, Southampton

Icons designed by Sarah Ward © 1994
Printed and bound in Great Britain

Contents

Preface IX
Acknowledgements XII

| 1 | Computers and VBA | 1 |

Introduction 2
Hardware and software 3
A brief history of computers 4
Microcomputer incompatibilities 7
Software and its evolution 8
Programming languages 12
Basic, Visual Basic and Excel 17
Visual Basic for Applications 19
Exercises 21

| 2 | Recorded Excel macros | 23 |

Introduction 24
The problem scenario 25
Creating a new macro 27
Working with macros 33
Macros for Excel charts 36
The Visual Basic toolbar 39
Macro security issues 40
Exercises 41

| 3 | Introduction to VBA | 43 |

Excel and VBA 44
The VBA environment 45
Structured English pseudocode 50
Input and output in VBA 52

Running VBA modules 57

Tips for running VBA macros 59

Calculations in VBA 61

VBA for Excel Help 63

Creating and naming a module 65

Exercises 66

4   Introduction to objects   67

Object-oriented programming 68

Object collections 71

The Excel object model 75

The Object Browser 77

Referencing named ranges 84

Exercises 89

5   Variables   91

What are variables? 92

Variable declarations 96

Explicit and implicit declarations 97

Assigning values to variables 99

VBA program using variables 101

Using constants in VBA 104

User-defined data types 105

Using arrays in VBA 107

Exercises 111

6   Decisions in VBA   113

Comparison operators 114

Comparing different data types 116

Logical operators 122

Select case 123

The operators in VBA 127

Exercises 128

7   Loops   129

For Each ... Next 130

For... Next loops 132

Exiting a For loop 137

Do ... Loop 139

Loop termination 143

Which loop structure is best? 144

Exercises 145

8   Debugging and testing   147

Types of programming errors 148

Testing and debugging 151

The Debug tools 154

The Immediate window 160

Maintenance of VBA programs 166

Exercises 167

9   Subs and functions   169

Subroutines 170

Functions 172

Creating functions 174

Passing parameters.. 182

Exercises 186

10 Using forms   187

User forms 188

The form design 194

Event procedures 199

Creating event procedure code 200

Creating context-sensitive Help 203

Designing for the end user 209

Exercises 212

Appendices   213

ASCII codes 214

Events 215

Further reading 219

Useful VBA websites 220

Index   221

Preface

Visual Basic Applications for Excel is a programming language well suited to beginners. It provides many of the Visual Basic programming facilities through the Excel application. Thus, students who have access to Excel can gain familiarity with Visual Basic without having to step up to the full blown program. With VBA, programmers have the power to customise Excel applications that would be impossible to achieve with Excel alone. VBA can often provide a faster, and sometimes easier-to-implement solution, than could be achieved with Excel alone. In particular, VBA gives you the power to automate all sorts of Excel tasks. For example, you could create an Excel workbook, add data to it and format it automatically using VBA. Excel is almost ubiquitous in the business world, and is amongst the most popular software applications ever used. These reasons make VBA for Excel an excellent choice as an introductory programming language.

I have tried to avoid pedantic use of technical programming and to concentrate instead on the understanding of core programming concepts. VBA is a large language, although much can be achieved by using only a small portion of its features. This book aims to give you a solid grasp of core principles and techniques, and an awareness of how to discover other language features so that you may learn them if and when required.

This book is ideally suited to undergraduate Business Information Technology students, although it could benefit students taking courses in Computer Science, Software Engineering, Business Studies and many other academic disciplines. It could also be beneficial to any student, without a technical computing background, looking for an introduction to programming. It could also be suitable for those who have used Excel and wish to acquire advanced knowledge about it. Some knowledge of Excel is required, but not of computer programming.

The book begins with an introductory chapter on computing. Readers who already have some understanding of computing software might skip parts, or all, of this chapter. It looks at the historical development of hardware and software and briefly describes the evolution of VBA and Excel and introduces readers to some of the jargon they will encounter in the world of programming. The chapter also outlines the advantages of using VBA for Excel.

Chapter 2 provides a general introduction to macros, and explains how to record and invoke macros without using the VBA language environment. It also looks at other ways of executing macros from Excel, such as by linking macros to buttons.

Chapter 3 introduces the VBA for Excel development environment and shows how to write and execute VBA macros. Once this chapter has been mastered, you will be able to distinguish how all the various parts of a VBA program and Excel go together to produce the working application.

Chapter 4 is about Excel objects. Object-oriented programming provides a way of developing software so that the relationship between the concepts of the real world system that is being modelled can be closely preserved within the software. It is important to introduce the concept of objects in the VBA language at an early stage, so that you can manipulate them when writing VBA macros. The VBA/Excel model contains objects such as workbooks, cell ranges, cells, and charts.

Chapter 5 deals with VBA variables and arrays. It gives many examples of how VBA supports both numeric and character data and introduced the mathematical operators that VBA recognises. This chapter also looks at user-defined variables.

It is sometimes desirable that some line(s) of code in a program are only executed if some condition is met. This is called *selection* and is the subject of Chapter 6. Logical operators for combining conditions will also be studied in this chapter.

Chapter 7 looks at the control structures for *iteration* – the repeating of lines of code in a program until some condition is met.

Chapter 8 discusses a range of testing and debugging facilities that are available in the VBA environment. The interactive debugger provides the tools to enable the student to know how to eliminate logical program errors. The chapter will also outline a test rationale and strategy for ensuring correctness of VBA programs, and look at VBA statements that control user input and other types of program error.

In Chapter 9 we look at functions. Excel users will be aware of the availability of a library of 'built-in' functions, such as those that find the total, average, or count the values of a column of data. These functions are also available to the VBA programmer, eliminating the need for coding repetitious tasks. VBA programmers can create their own functions and add them to the built-in function library of VBA, facilitating reuse and speeding up subsequent program development.

Chapter 10 is concerned with using *forms* in VBA programs, so that the reader will be able to create customised dialog boxes. Being a Windows-development system, VBA relies heavily on graphical screen objects, in this chapter, the reader will learn how to create and program windows components in an Excel application. This chapter will also look at other ways to improve the Excel user interface.

Writing this book has been a challenge and a pleasure. I hope that you find the same challenge and pleasure in learning to program in VBA.

Keith Darlington,

Summer 2003

Acknowledgements

I would like to thank my colleagues at South Bank University for their general support and comments. In particular, Dr Val Flynn and Kemi Adeboye. Many thanks also to Ian Edmonds whose excellent SBDS unit inspired this book. I would also like to thank the series editor Peter McBride for his invaluable support and help with this project and also Mike Cash, the publisher of the Made Simple series at Elsevier Publishing for his useful suggestions during the writing of this book. Finally, thanks to my wife Janice and to my three daughters Katie, Amy and Rhiannon for their patience and understanding during those many hours spent typing away at the keyboard.

To: Katie, Amy and Rhiannon

1 Computers and VBA

Introduction 2

Hardware and software 3

A brief history of computers 4

Microcomputer incompatibilities . . . 7

Software and its evolution 8

Programming languages 12

Basic, Visual Basic and Excel 17

Visual Basic for Applications 19

Exercises 21

Introduction

This book is about Visual Basic for Applications with Excel (VBA). VBA is one of many programming languages. This chapter provides the reader with a general understanding of programming languages and their evolution. If you know how and why programming concepts have evolved in the way in which they have, then you will have a better understanding of the way that basis tenets of computer programming fit together. In so doing, you should have enough to acquire and continue the development of programming skills.

Readers who already have some understanding of computing software might skip parts, or all, of this chapter. Those who don't will find this chapter useful in that it provides a meaning to many concepts that are explored in later chapters. The chapter looks at the historical development of hardware and software and briefly describes the evolution of VBA and Excel as well as introducing the reader to some of the jargon they will encounter in the world of programming. This should provide a good foundation for many of the concepts that the student will meet in later chapters.

Hardware and software

Every computer system contains hardware and software. Hardware refers to the physical components that make up a computer system. Software refers to the programs that operate the hardware. The hardware will normally consist such as the PC itself – called the base unit – as well as other devices connected to the base unit, such as the keyboard, mouse, printer, scanner, and so on. These devices are usually connected to the base unit by cables, or some other means. Input devices are devices that receive information from the user, such as a keyboard, scanner, microphone or mouse. Output devices, on the other hand, are devices that send information to the user, such as a display unit, printer, or sound speakers (see Figure 1.1). Devices connected to the base unit are collectively known as peripherals. The base unit contains, amongst other things, the Central Processing Unit (CPU), which is the 'brain' of the system, short-term memory and long-term memory in the form of hard disk drives, CDROM drives, zip drives, etc. Short-term memory comes in two main varieties on microcomputers: ROM and RAM. ROM is an acronym for Read Only Memory. As the name suggests, this type of memory is non-volatile and permanent. This means that ROM is never erased even when the computer is shut down. Its primary purpose is to store programs that are permanently required, some of which will be described in the later sections in this chapter. RAM is an acronym for Random Access Memory and is non-permanent volatile memory. Its purpose is for storing programs and data during the running of computer programs. RAM memory is erased when the computer is shut down.

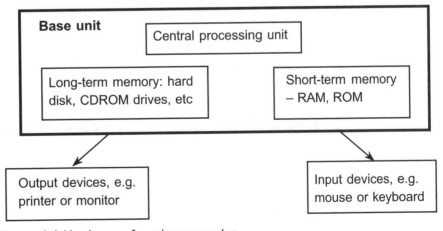

Figure 1.1 Hardware of a microcomputer

A brief history of computers

The development of computer hardware over the last 50 years has been remarkable with each generation becoming faster, cheaper, smaller and more powerful. Gordon Moore, co-founder of the Intel Corporation, predicted in 1965 that computer power, roughly speaking, would double every 18 months. This became known as Moore's Law and to this date has turned out to be remarkably accurate. To put the advance in perspective, the first electronic computers built in the late 1940s had been capable of a few hundred operations per second compared with computers that were built 50 years later capable of one trillion operations per second. Indeed, such has been the speed of change, that the processing power of a mobile telephone now exceeds that of the early generations of mainframe computers. The main reason has been the phenomenal advance in electronic technology in the manufacture of computer components. Since the first computers began to appear in the late 1940s, there have been four distinct generations of computer hardware characterised by advances in electronic technology.

The first generation

The first generation of electronic digital computers were built during the 1940s. They were known as mainframe computers. They were very large, difficult to use and extremely slow for they used vacuum tubes (or valves) for their operation. Machines of this generation were generally confined to academic and scientific uses in universities. Some notable systems were:

- The ENIAC computer – this was built at the University of Pennsylvania and came into use in 1946. It used a total of 18,000 electronic valves. It also consumed an area of space roughly equivalent to half a football field, weighed 30 tons, and performed about 300 multiplications of two 10-digit numbers per second.

- The Harvard Mark 1 – developed at Harvard University in 1945, the Mark 1 was capable of one multiplication every 3 seconds. The term 'debugging' (see Chapter 8) originated here when one of the computer scientists discovered a moth fused to the circuitry causing the machine to malfunction.

The second generation

The second generation of computers emerged during the 1950s and were characterised by the use of transistor components, which were also known for their use in radios – transistor radios – during this time. They were a significant improvement on valves, for they were considerably smaller, faster, more reliable and less expensive. Transistor components then were huge by comparison with the current generation. However, they were a step-up from the valve generation because second-generation machines were much faster, smaller and had greater memory capacities. It was during this period that the digital computer were first being used for business applications, such as producing the weekly payroll and other mundane tasks which, hitherto, would have been done manually. Examples include:

- Leo – a computer system built in the early 1950s by the Lyons Tea Company. It was the first computer ever to be used for company data processing tasks.
- The IBM 701 EPDM – this was the first mainframe computer system built by the computer giant IBM .

The third generation

The third generation of computers emerged during the mid-1960s and were based upon integrated circuit technology. Integrated circuits provided significant reduction in size over transistors. Minicomputers evolved from integrated circuit technology. These were smaller and cheaper than mainframes but delivered similar processor power, although were often of lower storage capacities. Minicomputers became affordable systems and were purchased in large numbers by organisations such as universities and other higher education institutes, as well as industrial, commercial and government organisations. Examples of systems that were built during this time were:

- The DEC PDP 8 minicomputer – this was a very popular computer system during the 1970s and provided multi-tasking facilities that enabled several people to use the system at the same time.
- The DEC PDP 11 – this was an even more popular minicomputer than the DEC PDP 8.

The fourth generation

The fourth generation of computers became known as microcomputers, and were being built in the late 1970s and were based upon silicon chip technology. The level of miniaturisation was such that these silicon chip based machines became small enough to fit on a home desktop and, thus, the birth of the home computer began. The term microcomputer has now become synonymous with what we now call the Personal Computer (PC). Today's machines are still using silicon chip technology, but, enormously powerful compared to the early crop of silicon chip machines. Examples of early fourth-generation computers were:

- The Apple II microcomputer – developed by Steve Jobs and Steve Wozniak, co-founders of the Apple Corporation, during 1978. The Apple II was a huge success with worldwide sales exceeding 1 million. The system used an 8-bit Motorola 6502 microprocessor, had 16k standard RAM memory and used floppy disks for external storage. The Apple II was priced at under $2000, and became a leader in the educational and home computing markets, as well as the small business sector.

- The BBC Micro manufactured by Acorn Computers, this was a very successful UK microcomputer during the early 1980s. The system had 32k RAM standard memory and used magnetic tape cassette medium for storage, although it was expandable to include floppy disk storage. It was successful both in the home and educational computing markets, with many schools and college using networked BBC Micros.

Microcomputer incompatibilities

Despite the growing markets in microcomputers in the early 1980s, mass market penetration was limited partly because of the lack of compatibility between different computer systems. For example, a printer compatible with one microcomputer would be unlikely to work on one made by another manufacturer. The same problem arose with software: programs written to work on one microcomputer would not run on any other system. There was little compatibility because there was no standard system in operation. This gave software developers little incentive to invest heavily in programs that were destined to deliver limited returns. All of this was about to change when, in 1981, the mainframe computer giant IBM introduced the IBM PC.

The IBM PC – the catalyst for standards

By the time that the fourth-generation computers were being built, IBM was well established in manufacturing mainframe and minicomputers. IBM's entry into the microcomputer market was relatively late, but turned out to be a defining moment because the IBM PC became a standard. It did so in the sense that other computer manufacturers were keen to ensure that software written for their systems would work on the IBM PC: they wanted to ensure that their software was 'IBM compatible'. This created a bandwagon effect with manufacturers everywhere building IBM-compatible machines. It also gave software developers the incentive they needed and spawned the development of high quality business software such as the spreadsheet Lotus 123 (see later in this chapter). When IBM released the PC, they enlisted the Microsoft Corporation to write the operating system called DOS (Disk Operating System) for the PC and this also became a standard. They also enlisted the microprocessor company Intel to incorporate the 16-bit 8086 microprocessor into their computer. This processor evolved into the 80486, which was replaced by the Pentium processor in the mid-1990s.

The impact of the IBM was such that the PC market became segmented into those that were IBM compatible; and those that were not. The Apple Macintosh computer was developed in 1984, and is the only survivor of that generation that was not IBM compatible. PC computer sales rocketed during the 1990s. Current estimates suggest there are over now 500 million personal computers used in the world.

Software and its evolution

(handwritten: TASK)

(handwritten: program, operation)

Computer hardware is of little use without computer software: hardware without software is like a CD player without compact disks. However, the hardware of a computer system requires different types of software – called programs – to operate. First, it needs programs that will control all the hardware units to link together so that they act as a whole, and enable the user to interact with the computer. The software to operate and control the hardware is called the *operating system* or *operating system software*. Second, it needs programs to perform a specific task, such as enable the user to send an e-mail message, or create a balance account using a spreadsheet. These programs are called *application programs*, or *application software*. Application and system programs are collectively known as software.

Operating system software

The most important item of system software running on any computer is the operating system. Its role is to provide the services and manage the resources so that the user can interact with the hardware. This will include providing the means to enable various applications that are stored on the hard disk of the PC to be run when required. The operating system will also interact with other devices in tasks such as accessing a CD ROM, or a scanner when it is needed for use. Common examples of operating systems that run on a PC are UNIX, Linux, DOS, and Windows XP.

The first generation mainframe operating system software was generally controlled by one job at a time called batch processing. Huge decks of punched cards or reels of paper tape were used to do this, which was extremely slow. Added to that, processing was usually centralized in some company center, thus program submissions would take days to process. As computers became more powerful in terms of speed and memory, so operating system software became more sophisticated, enabling more than one task to be processed at one time. This was known as multiprocessing and made more efficient use of the computer's resources because the operating system could be programmed to control the simultaneous operation of many jobs in the computer. The concept of timesharing quickly followed on both mainframes and minicomputers from the 1970s. Timesharing allowed for several terminal users to be connected to the computer, possible via remote connections, and gain access to the central processing unit through a time slice. This time slice could be allocated to thousands of on-line users simultaneously. However, because of the speed of the computer, the user would not be aware of this and would feel they were getting dedicated service.

The microcomputer DOS operating system

When the mainframe computer giant IBM entered the PC market in 1981, the Microsoft Corporation were enlisted to write the operating system called MS DOS or DOS (Disk Operating System). DOS had evolved from CP/M (Control Processor for Microcomputers) – an operating system written in the 1970s for 8-bit microprocessors. The DOS operating system was a single tasking – meaning only one task could be processed at a time – and single user operating system. DOS therefore, only utilised a small proportion of the computing power of the PC. It used a 'command driven interface' by which is meant that that users communicated with DOS by typing commands directly through the keyboard (see Figure 1.2). Learning to use DOS was time-consuming and involved a great deal of effort compared with the Windows operating system which followed it. Users of DOS had to learn many commands before they could become competent computer users.

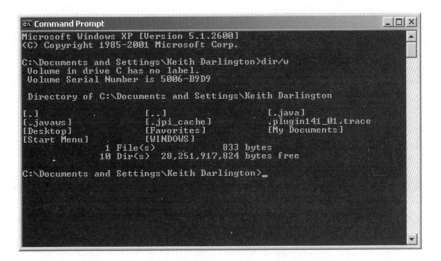

Figure 1.2 Illustration of the DOS user interface

The Windows operating system

Other operating systems attempted to overcome the shortcomings of DOS during the late 1980s including the IBM Operating System/2 (OS/2), and UNIX. Both were moderately successful, but it was the release of Microsoft Windows 3.0 in 1990 which triggered the beginning of the end of the dominance of DOS. Windows 3.0 used a graphic user interface (GUI) based environment. The first microcomputer providing a GUI interface was the Apple Macintosh, first manufactured in 1984.

A GUI based operating system makes life much easier for the user because rather than typing commands from the keyboard, the user can perform tasks by clicking graphical icons, or other controls with the use of the mouse. In the Microsoft Windows environment, application programs such as a calculator program could be invoked, by clicking the calc icon (see Figure 1.3). This application would then appear in a program window (hence the name 'Windows' given to the operating system). Notice how the calculator application window has appeared below the Calculator icon in the illustration (this is not always the case). Windows 3.0 sold over 30 million copies worldwide – a huge success! However, it contained many program bugs, and a more stable and successful version called Windows 3.1 was released in 1991. Windows 3.1 was the forerunner to Windows 95, Windows 98 and Windows XP, which was released in late 2001.

During the mid-1990s, when the Windows operating system software began to replace the DOS operating system, the term IBM compatible became synonymous with Windows compatible. The personal computer market segmented between Windows compatible and Macintosh compatible systems. However, Windows systems maintain market dominance with more than 90 per cent market share as of the time of writing this book.

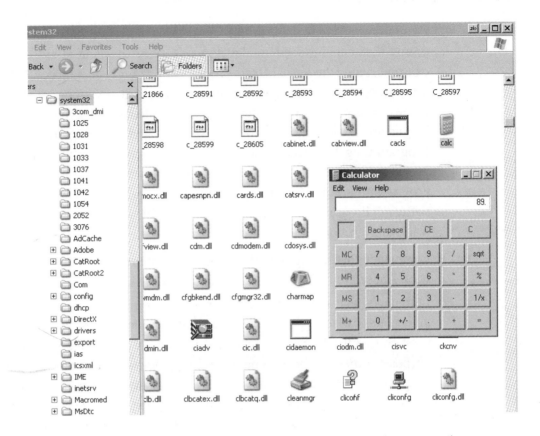

Figure 1.3 Opening an application program in the Windows operating system

~~TASK.~~

Application software

Application software is primarily used for developing specific applications, such as producing a company report, or maintaining a medical database. Programs such as Microsoft Word or Access could be used for developing these. These are examples of application specific programs; Access is specifically used for database applications, while Word is specifically used for word-processing applications. Applications can also be developed using programming languages.

Programming languages

Programming languages, unlike application software, are software programs that can be used to develop a variety of stand-alone tasks. For example, using the Visual Basic programming language, you could develop a program to help managers to make investment decisions, or develop a games program, or something like a daily planner, or even, with certain languages, something that controls some aspect of the operating system. Programming languages bear little resemblance to spoken languages for programming languages have to be precise and unambiguous. Hence, programming languages require a longer learning curve than application software. Programming languages are, roughly speaking, classified into the following groups:

- Languages that manipulate the operating system or the hardware in some way. These are called system languages, or low-level languages.

- Languages that are used to develop stand-alone applications. These languages are called high-level languages. Examples are: Visual Basic, Java, C++ and COBOL. Some high-level languages are developed for special purposes, others are general purpose: COBOL is a special-purpose business language, while Java is widely regarded as an Internet language and Visual Basic and C++ are both general-purpose languages. These languages could be, and in many cases have been, used to produce software applications such as the word processor program Word, or the spreadsheet program Excel.

- Languages that are designed to enhance the capabilities of application software. For example, Excel uses *VBA* to enhance its capabilities, while *VBA for Word* enhances the capabilities of Word. Typically, these languages would be used to expand the capabilities of the software that would be very difficult – if not impossible – to do within the application itself.

Evolution of programming languages and VBA

Computer software, like hardware, has advanced through many generations since the birth of the digital computer. The early machines lacked the speed and power and the software available at that time was sufficient. However, as hardware became more powerful and sophisticated, so the software needed to exploit that power to achieve maximum benefit. This section looks at the stages of evolution of computer software.

First-generation languages (machine code)

The first generation of digital computers that were built in the late-1940s used program code that was written in binary – sequences of 1s and 0s, or BITs (BInary digiTs). This was known as machine code. It was very difficult to understand and the programmer needed to have a great deal of knowledge about the hardware of the system in order to write programs. Even something which seems quite simple, such as transferring a byte of data from memory to a register (temporary storage on the CPU) took a great deal of effort. This low-level programming was very time-consuming, easy for the programmer to make mistakes, and it was very difficult to understand the code and required very many low-level instructions to carry out even the simplest of operations.

Second-generation languages (assembler languages)

Assembler languages began to replace machine code in the early 1950s. The main difference between these and machine code was that the machine code was assembled into instructions, which were given mnemonic names to make them easier for the programmer to remember. These instructions would then be translated into machine code by a program called an 'assembler': hence the name assembler languages.

Third-generation languages (high-level languages)

Third-generation languages (3GL), also became known as high-level languages and were written in such a way that single statement would be converted into several low level machine instructions. A translator program would then be used that would convert the high-level instructions into machine language. Such a program is called a *compiler* although some languages – VB included – use an *interpreter* (interpreters will be discussed later in the chapter). A compiler is a program that translates high-level source code into machine language and creates an executable file: i.e. a file that can be executed directly from the operating system.

Many 3GLs were developed for special purposes, and began to appear in the mid-1950s. FORTRAN (FORmula TRANslation) was the first of the crop developed by IBM in 1954 for scientific purposes. COBOL (COmmon Business Oriented Language) was developed in 1959 for commercial applications. Pascal, developed in 1971, was primarily developed for educational purposes. A variety of high-level languages were created for different kinds of tasks. Each one provides different kinds of abstractions for the different tasks they were created to solve. Thus, FORTRAN was strong on scientific abstractions and number crunching, making it an ideal scientific language. COBOL on the other hand was very strong on file handling and reporting; making it an ideal business language. Pascal was strong on structured programming to facilitate good program practice and therefore became popular as an educational language. C was another very popular general purpose high-level language. The thing that made C so popular was that it provided low-level language and high-level facilities making it relatively fast to compile programs.

Fourth-generation languages (visual languages)

Fourth-generation languages (4GL) provide a higher level of abstraction than third-generation languages in that they support visual program development. With visual programming, the programmer has the ability to create graphical user interfaces by pointing and clicking with a mouse, similar to using the Windows operating system. This contrasts with third-generation programming where the programmer has to write code with the keyboard. 4GLs are a product of the visual programming age that began with the rise of the GUI operating systems such as Windows. 4GLs have many recognised features including:

- Rapid development of applications compared to 3GLs
- Visual environment for development
- Built-in 3GL language support
- Faster learning curve

Visual Basic, and even VBA for Excel to a certain extent, is a 4GL that evolved from Microsoft Basic which was used on the first-generation microcomputers. With Visual Basic, programs are created in an Integrated Development Environment (IDE). The IDE provides a means of producing programs in a fraction of the time it would take using a 3GL. Delphi is another fourth-generation Windows programming language that was developed by the Borland company in the early 1990s. Delphi evolved from a very successful DOS version of Pascal, called Turbo Pascal, developed in 1984. 3GL language support is an essential feature of a 4GL as the developer can only do so much with the 4GL visual layer. The Delphi visual programmer's interface is shown in Figure 1.8, and is similar to that used in Visual Basic. The illustration displays a Form that the developer can drop components onto as the means of developing the application. The important point to make is that although this can be achieved visually, the developer will often have to program at the 3GL level, as we will see in Chapter 10. The main difference between Visual Basic and Delphi is that the former is an *interpreted* language. An interpreted language translates source code line by line; by contrast Delphi is a compiled 4GL, which means the code is completely translated into machine language before execution. Therefore, the program will run faster if compiled. Both Visual Basic and Delphi are Rapid Application Development (RAD) languages.

Fifth-generation languages (artificial intelligence languages)

Fifth-generation languages were characterised by *artificial intelligence* (AI). The term 'fifth-generation' became established during the 1980s. These languages are not, contrary to popular belief, the sequel to 4GLs. AI languages use a different paradigm to previous generations. Previous generations used the procedural programming paradigm to solve a problem: this paradigm works by knowing 'how to solve the problem'. On the other hand, AI programs use the declarative paradigm: this solves a problem by knowing 'what the problem is' and then using in-built logic programming capabilities to reason facts and draw conclusions. The two most commonly used AI languages are Lisp and Prolog.

Object-oriented programming languages

Object-oriented programming (OOP) languages have had a major impact on software development in the last decade. The OOP idea began to ferment in the 1970s, but it was not until the emergence of the Windows operating system that OOP languages became an established program paradigm. The main benefit of OOP is that programs become more re-usable. Software objects can limit and control a computer program and the data on which it

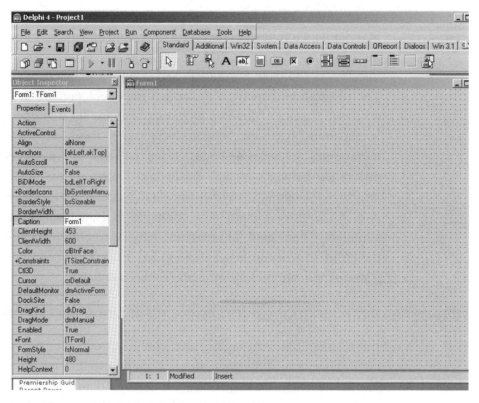

Figure 1.4 Illustration of the Delphi Interface

operated. It would allow programmers access to the data only in the way that was intended by the original programmer, so that there would be a smaller risk of any harmful side-effects to the data. The first pure OOP language was Smalltalk, but far more successful, was the OOP high-level language called C++. This was developed by Bjarne Stroustrup in the late 1980s and evolved from the C language. C programmers could easily migrate to C++ because the only difference between the two was that C++ contained object-oriented extensions. Other high level language vendors followed suit with object-based versions of Pascal, Prolog, and Basic.

Basic, Visual Basic and Excel

To understand how VBA for Excel evolved, we need to understand something about the evolution of both programming language Visual Basic and the Windows spreadsheet software application Excel.

Basic and Visual Basic

Visual Basic evolved from the third-generation language called Basic (Beginners All Purpose Instruction Code). This was originally developed at Dartmouth College in 1965 on a mainframe computer. Its primary purpose at that time was as an educational language and it was intended to be used as a stepping-stone for students to learn a more advanced language, such as ALGOL. However, the status of Basic changed rapidly when it became the established language for the first wave of microcomputers. In the late 1970s, Bill Gates and Paul Allen, created a version of Basic which was ideally suited to 8-bit microcomputers. Bill Gates and Paul Allen formed the Microsoft Corporation with Microsoft Basic becoming available on a range of microcomputers such as the Apple, the BBC Micro and the Commodore range.

Basic was a language that was perfectly suited to the microcomputer because of its small memory requirements compared to other languages. Moreover, Basic was an interpreted language, and was easier to use than compiled languages such as FORTRAN and COBOL. However, Basic also had severe critics: especially in the academic community. Basic was seen to be encouraging 'bad programming habits'; the main culprit being the dreaded 'Go To' statement that was part of the Basic language. This statement was seen as anathema to good structured programming skills because programmers could use this statement to do anything without regard to good programming style and structure. Nevertheless, Microsoft continued their commitment to the development to Basic alongside the DOS operating system during the 1980s. A major revision of Basic was undertaken in the early 1990s to enable it to work under the then new Windows operating system. Basic became Visual Basic – so-called because it supports many of the visually based drag and drop graphic user interface operations that are prevalent in the Windows operating system. Visual Basic version 1 was released in 1991 and experienced rapid version changes that roughly reflected the changes in the Windows operating system itself during the next decade. Visual Basic has now established itself as a very successful stand-alone visual programming language.

Excel and macros

The idea of a spreadsheet software application was first developed in a program called VisiCalc that was commercially available in the late 1970s. It was developed by Dan Bricklin and Bob Frankston and written for the Apple II micro and many believed, at the time, that it had a major impact on the success of the Apple.

It was not until the arrival of Lotus 1-2-3 however, that spreadsheets really make an impact in the business environment. Lotus 1-2-3 was released in January 1983 by the Lotus Development Corporation for use on the IBM PC, and proved to be a huge success. The success of Lotus 1-2-3 was partly due to its macro capability because macros gave developers a means of automating repetitive tasks that are commonplace in the business environment. Microsoft was also marketing spreadsheet software during this time with a product called MultiPlan that was written for the CP/M operating system.

The Excel spreadsheet program evolved from MultiPlan when it was first released in 1985. It was released for use on the Apple Macintosh. However, Microsoft carried the macro concept further than Lotus 1-2-3 by introducing a macro language, called XLM. Macros created in this way would be stored in a macro sheet that was separate from the worksheet and stored with a filename with an .xlm extension. These were known as XLM macros (or Excel 5 macros), and while they provided something far superior to their competitors, such as Lotus 123, XLM macros lacked any unifying structure to enable them to work with other Microsoft programs, such as Word or PowerPoint.

Visual Basic for Applications

Excel, like Visual Basic, experienced several revisions during the 1990s, roughly in-line with the changes to the Windows operating system, but Excel 5, released in early 1994, included the first version of VBA. This was a big step forward for VBA was intended to unify the programming code behind the Microsoft Office application program suite. Office was originally released to run on Windows 3.1, and contained a suite of programs including: Word, Excel, Outlook and Access.

Following the early success of VBA, Microsoft decided to incorporate VBA into Access (the database application). By the time Office 97 was released, VBA had made its way into four of the five Office applications: Word, Access, Excel and PowerPoint. The fifth Office 97 application, Outlook contained VBScript – a variant of the Visual Basic language widely used for Internet applications.

VBA is a programming language created by Microsoft that can be built into applications. For example, VBA for Excel is a programming language that is contained within Excel. It primary purpose is to enhance and automate applications that use Excel. VBA is based on the stand-alone Visual Basic language but works within some other Microsoft application.

There are many advantages for incorporating VBA into applications.

- Given the diverse requirements and demands of end users, it is often almost impossible for off-the-shelf applications to deliver 100 percent of user requirements. VBA can often complement the facilities within the software application often offering a better solution.

- Applications that host the VBA language can be customised to meet user requirements and integrated with other VBA-enabled applications on the desktop. Thus, Microsoft Office applications share a common tool for customization with VBA.

- Solutions created with Visual Basic for Applications execute faster since they run in the same memory space as the host application and are tightly integrated with the application. This allows developers to write code that responds to user actions, such as when a user opens, closes, saves and modifies documents or projects.

- VBA is highly compatible with Visual Basic. VBA is built from the same source code base as Visual Basic; therefore providing a high level of compatibility. VBA also uses the same high-performance language engine and programmer productivity tools as VB.

- VBA is becoming ubiquitous in the programming community For VBA is a language found in both Microsoft and non-Microsoft products. Indeed, the number of third-party software vendors who are licensing VBA to run with their products is growing rapidly. For more information on VBA future development visit the website:www.msdn.microsoft.com/vba/default.

VBA Excel version compatibility

When Microsoft introduced Excel 97, some radical changes to both the language and the developers interface were made. Excel 97 was the first time that Active X components could be embedded with worksheets and user forms. Compatibility with previous versions of VBA is far less likely than with versions released after Excel 97. At the time of writing this book, these include Excel 2000 and Excel XP. The VBA macros written in this book should work with versions of Excel 97 onwards. However, sometimes reference will be made to commands that were developed for Excel 5.

VB and VBA

VBA is not to be confused with Visual Basic; Visual Basic is a stand-alone program that runs independently. VBA, on the other hand, is part of an Office application, and therefore cannot work without the Office application. For example, VBA for Excel is part of the Excel program, and cannot run without Excel. There are many similarities in the language constructs however, and as already stated VBA is highly compatible with VB.

Exercises

1 State the elements of hardware that make up a microcomputer system. Give examples of each element.

2 Briefly describe the four generations of computer hardware, with an example from each generation.

3 Give three examples of 8 bit microcomputers.

4 What are the main factors attributed to the success of the IBM PC?

5 What is the main difference between hardware and software? Give an example of microcomputer hardware and software.

6 Categorise the following items as either operating system software or application software

       a) Windows 98

       b) Windows 3.1

       c) Excel

       d) OS/2

       e) WordPad

       f) Access

       g) Delphi

7 What is the difference between machine code and an assembler programming language?

8 What is the difference between a high-level and low-level programming language.

9 Give an example of a third-generation language and a fourth-generation language.

10 What is a fifth-generation programming language? Give an example.

11 Why was the fourth-generation language Basic regarded as anathema to the acquisition of structured programming skills?

12 What is the difference between a compiler and an interpreter? Give an example of a high-level language that is compiled and one that is interpreted.

13 What is the difference between VB and VBA?

14 What is the difference between a third- and a fourth-generation language? Give an example of each.

2 Recorded Excel macros

Introduction 24

The problem scenario 25

Creating a new macro 27

Working with macros 33

Macros for Excel charts 36

The Visual Basic toolbar 39

Macro security issues 40

Exercises 41

Introduction

Most people who use computer software will find themselves having to repeat a process of steps to perform some task. For example, an Excel user might have to update a worksheet every week with the weekly expenses. The task might involve a series of operations which are repeated every time the task becomes necessary, such as copying a cell range of data, pasting, clearing, saving, and many other possibilities. A macro provides a way of recording these operations so that the user does not have to retype all the same sequence of tasks each time. A macro is a sequence of commands that can run automatically within an application such as Excel or Word. A macro is often referred to as a procedure. The commands that can be performed with a macro include any operation that can be performed within that application.

Take note

You can use the **Name** command in the **Insert** menu to create a mnemonic name for a cell range, such as D1:E15. These named ranges can be referred to by the chosen name. Using named ranges is strongly recommended because it is much easier to understand the meaning of a named range than the standard cell range reference. Once you have created a named range, it will then be visible in the Name box which appears to the left of the Formula bar. You can see from Figure 2.1, that the range of cells called *month_no* has been currently selected. This range consists only of the cell B29.

The problem scenario

Throughout much of this book, we will be referring to an Excel workbook called SALESMAN.XLS. This contains a number of worksheets including that displayed in Figure 2.1. The purpose of this worksheet is to maintain weekly sales data for each representative employed by a sales company. The top section contains administrative data such as the date the worksheet was written, and so on. The lower section contains data showing a column of representative names, along with the total sales to date, then the grey shaded region that contains weekly sales data for each of four weeks (per month), the next column contains the monthly total for these weekly sales, the next column shows the monthly bonus earned by the corresponding representative, and finally, an end of month sales column. This is defined as the sales to date plus the end of month sales.

The following named ranges have been set in the *weeklysales* worksheet.

```
end_month_sales = I32:I40
month_bonus = H32:H40
month_total = G32:G40
week_sales = C32:F40
sales_to_date = B32:B40
rep_name = A32:A40
month_no = B29
bonus_rate = B28
```

Throughout this book, we will use many examples that are based upon the SALESMAN workbook. The file is available for downloading from the Made Simple website at: http//:www.madesimple.co.uk. Alternatively, you can create this file yourself, but make sure that it is identical to that shown in Figure 2.1 and includes the same named ranges.

Reasons for using macros

♦   *Executing repetitive tasks*   Many Excel business tasks require frequent repetition of some keyboard or mouse operations. For example, updating a company car expenses monthly spreadsheet might involve copying a range of cells to another, followed by clearing a range ready for next month's entry, followed by updating the total sales to date. A macro can be created to represent a task like this and then invoked whenever required; perhaps saving a great deal of time to the user who would otherwise have to retype the whole task over and over again whenever it is to be used.

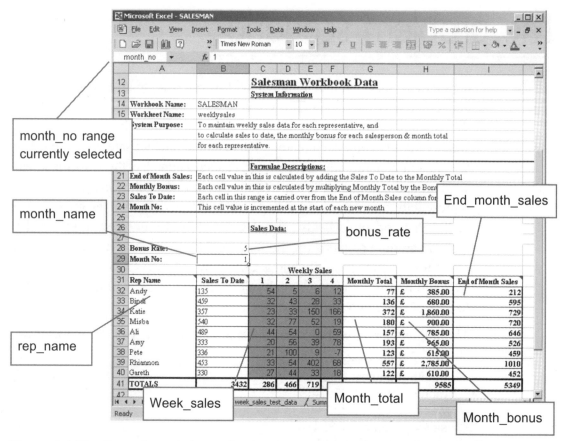

Figure 2.1 The Scenario worksheet, showing the named ranges

- *Input validation* Data may require validation. For example, when a number that represents a person's age is entered, anything outside the range 0 to 120 would probably be unacceptable. A macro can be used to ensure that data entered into a range of cells is restricted within this specified range of values.

- *User interface control* Many novice Excel users can feel overwhelmed by the complexity of using spreadsheets, even when just entering data. A macro can provide a friendlier interface that may include helpful dialog boxes. For example, a data entry clerk may work more efficiently by using a customised interface from a macro instead of entering data directly into the sheet.

- *Decision-making* A spreadsheet is a matrix of cell locations that can contain values, formulae and relationships. The key point to note is that all of the elements in the matrix are changed automatically when one or more of the assumptions are changed. This facility allows a series of outcomes to be explored, providing answers to 'what-if' questions that are an essential part of decision making. Macros can be created for this purpose.

Creating a new macro

There are two ways of creating an Excel VBA macro. They are:

◆ Record operations performed on worksheet;

◆ Type the macro source code in directly; that is using the VBA language.

The remainder of this chapter will focus on the first method. Chapter 3 will explore the VBA method.

Creating a macro by recording actions

Preparation is essential before recording a new macro. First, it should be noted that macros could involve many steps. These steps should be practised before recording the macro, because once the macro recorder begins, all the actions are recorded – mistakes as well. The macro recorder does not however, record the time taken between steps, so take your time to make sure that you don't have to repeat the process. Second, thought must be given to the environment for which the macro will operate. For example, will the macro be used for a specific document or a group of documents? If you are likely to open the macro with a specific workbook, then open the workbook. Otherwise, you might need to think about where it is likely to be used before recording a new macro. When these preparatory steps have been completed, the user can then proceed with recording.

You will need to do the following to record a new macro:

1 Set up the starting conditions for the macro, such as opening the workbook, and anything else that might be necessary. For example, it may be necessary to select a specific worksheet, or range of cells, etc.

Take note

Throughout the book, you may find that the items displayed on your system do not accord exactly with the screenshots. Don't panic if this is the case. It might be due to some interface modification in your version of Excel or other reasons.

2   From Excel, start the macro recorder by selecting the **Tools** menu, then selecting **Macro**, followed by the **Record New Macro** option (see Figure 2.2). In future, Excel commands like this will be written in following shorthand format: **Tools > Macro > Record New Macro**.

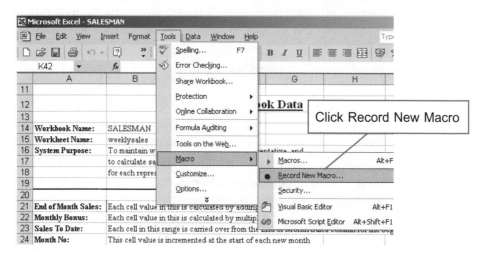

Figure 2.2 Selecting Record Macro from the Excel menu

3   The dialog box as shown in Figure 2.3 will appear. You should then enter a name for the new macro. Enter the name: *updateSalesRep*. Note also that you are invited to type in a description of what the macro does. It is customary to write the name of the person who wrote the macro, the date it was written, and the version number to facilitate future maintenance. From this dialog box you decide where the macro is to be stored by using the **Store macro in** drop-down list. If **This Workbook** is selected, then the macro will be stored in the current workbook only. If you select the option **Personal Macro Workbook** from the list, this has the effect of creating a global macro: meaning that it will be available to all workbooks created in Excel. Beware

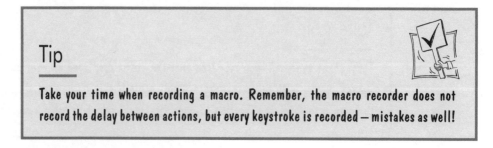

Tip

Take your time when recording a macro. Remember, the macro recorder does not record the delay between actions, but every keystroke is recorded — mistakes as well!

of saving a macro in the **Personal Macro Workbook** format because of the extra memory consumed. The **Shortcut key** box can be used to assign a keyboard shortcut to a macro, bear in mind however, that many of the **[Ctrl]** key combinations are already in use by the Excel system. Click **OK** when complete to start recording. The Record Macro Toolbar appears on the worksheet and the message 'Recording' will be visible in the bottom left hand side of the Status Bar.

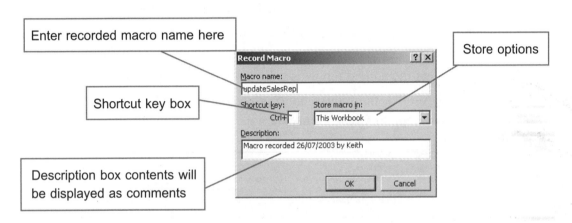

Figure 2.3 The Record Macro dialog box

Take note

The default name assigned to a new macro is Macro1. However, you should always change this to a more meaningful name. If you assign a name to a macro, it must conform to these rules:

+ Any macro name must begin with an alphabetical character

+ A macro name can be up to 255 characters long

+ A macro name can only contain numerical digits, alphabetic letters, and the underscore character (but not spaces or other punctuation characters).

4   Perform the actions that are to be recorded. These are:

♦ Open the workbook called SALESMAN.XLS

♦ Select the worksheet called *weeklysales*.

♦ Select the named range of cells *end_month_sales* (I32:I40). Note the selected range should appear in the **Name** box.

♦ Click the **Copy** button on the Standard toolbar.

♦ Select the top cell in the named range of cells *sales_to_date* (B32).

♦ Select **Edit > Paste Special**, and from the **Paste Special** dialog box, click **Values**.

♦ Select the named range of cells *week_sales* (C32:F40).

♦ Right-click the mouse button over the selected range and choose the menu option **Clear Contents**.

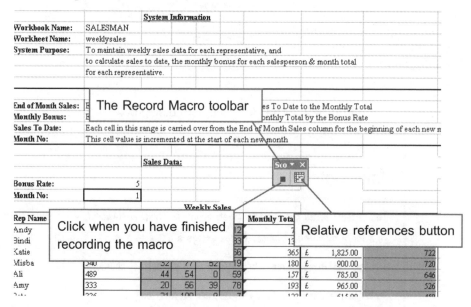

Figure 2.4   Selecting the range end_month_sales in the worksheet 'weeklysales'

5   When all the steps in the macro are complete, stop the macro recorder. To do this, click the **Stop** button on the Record Macro toolbar. Check the Status Bar no longer says 'Recording'. Note that it is not necessary to save the macro. The macro is now ready to be executed when required.

Dealing with cell references in macros

All cell references are absolute references by default. This means that if a cell is clicked during macro recording, the macro selects the exact cell each time that the macro is played back (invoked). To instruct Excel to use relative references, click the **Use Relative References** button on the Macro toolbar.

Executing a macro from Excel

Before executing a macro for the first time, you should save anything currently open just in case the macro contains mistakes that were made during recording. The playback results may not be as expected. In the event of errors in the macro, it can be rerecorded using the same name. The steps involved in running the macro are then as follows:

1   From a worksheet, select **Tools > Macro > Macros** to see the **Macro** dialog box (see Figure 2.5).

2   Select the macro name from the list using the cursor keys, and then click on the Run button. The macro will execute one step at a time and return control to the user when complete. As you can see from the screenshot in Figure 2.6, the macro has performed the actions required.

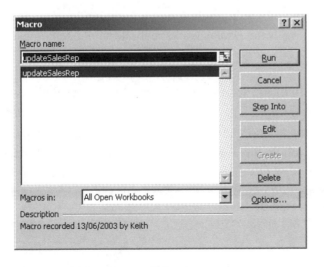

Tip

Always make sure that your data is saved, or that you have a backup file, before executing any new macros that you have created. Otherwise if your macro crashes you might not be able to recover it.

Figure 2.5 The Macro dialog box

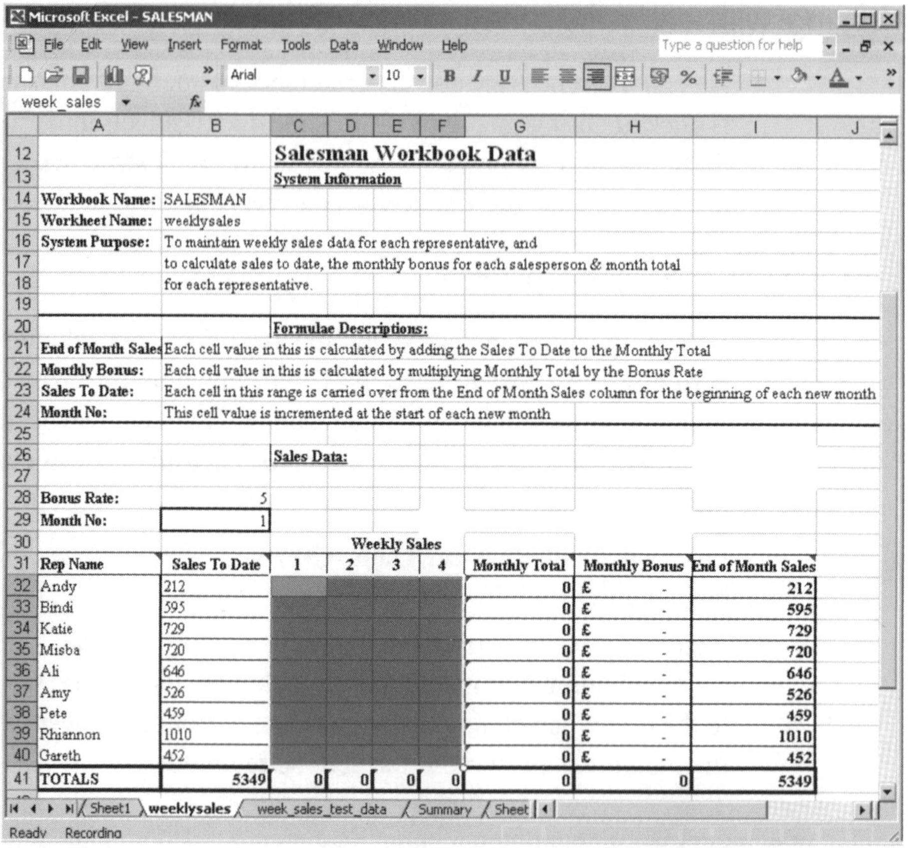

Figure 2.6 Screenshot of *weeklysales* worksheet after the macro is executed

The week_sales_test_data worksheet

The tabs at the bottom of the screenshot (Figure 2.6) shows there is a sheet called *week_sales_test_data*. This holds test data so that you can rerun the macros without having to enter new data every time. To reload data into the *weekly_sales* range, click the *week_sales_test_data* sheet and select the range *testdata*. Copy and paste it into *week_sales* in the *weeklysales* sheet.

Take note

You cannot select a macro button by simply clicking it, as that will execute the macro, instead, hold [Ctrl] as you click. You can then move, resize or rename it as required.

Working with macros

Linking a button to a macro

To run a macro from the macro dialog box, the user must be aware that the macro exists, and several keystrokes are required to invoke it! As an alternative, you can linked a macro to a button – that can be placed anywhere on a sheet. Users can then invoke a macro by simply clicking the button.

To link a button to the *updateSalesRep* macro:

1   Select the *weeklysales* worksheet from the SALESMAN workbook.

2   Select **View** > **Toolbars** > **Forms** to display the Forms toolbar on the worksheet. Make sure the worksheet is unprotected, otherwise the Forms toolbar will be greyed out.

3   Click the **Button** icon on the Forms toolbar, then click on the worksheet where you will want this to appear. You will then see the **Assign Macro** dialog box. To assign an existing macro to the button or graphic control, enter the name of the macro in the **Macro name**: field, and click **OK**.

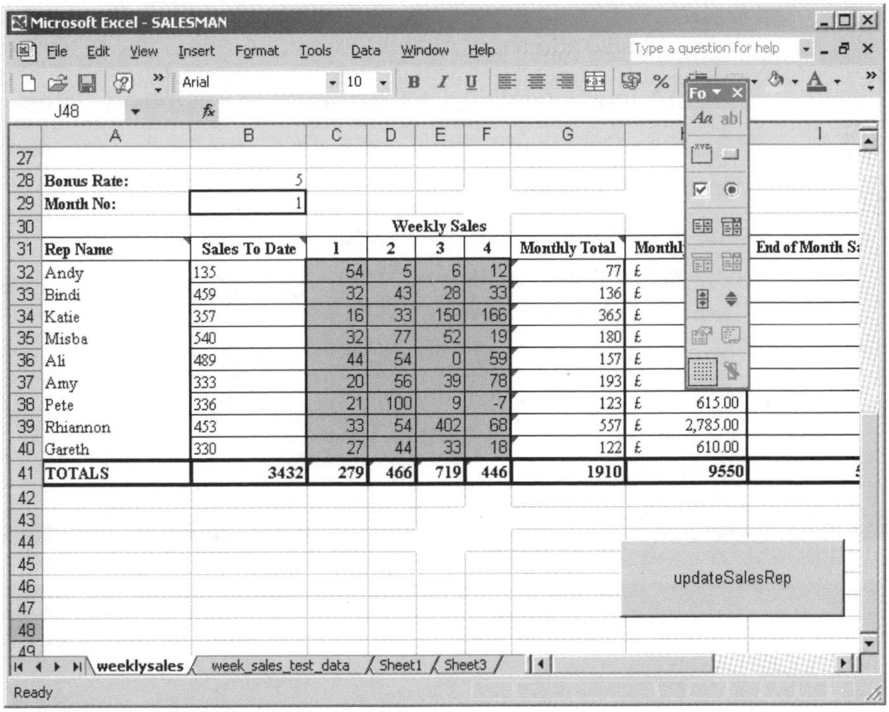

Figure 2.7 The button *updateSalesRep* on the *weeklysales* worksheet.

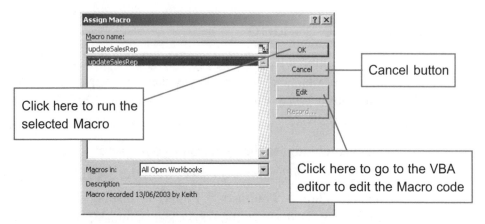

Figure 2.8 The Assign Macro dialog box

4   Resize and name the button. Move the cursor to some other point on the worksheet and click to deselect the button. Its appearance will be similar to that in Figure 2.7. The button can now be used to run the macro.

Adding macros to a toolbar

You can also add a macro to a toolbar, or assign one to a customised button.

1   Select **View > Toolbars > Customise** to open the **Customise** dialog box.

2   Click the **Commands** tab to open the **Commands** page, and select **Macros** from the **Categories** list (see Figure 2.9).

3   The **Commands** list for macros has two options: **Custom Menu Item** and **Custom Button**. To add the macro to a toolbar, choose **Custom Button**, and drag it into place, e.g. on the Standard toolbar (see Figure 2.10).

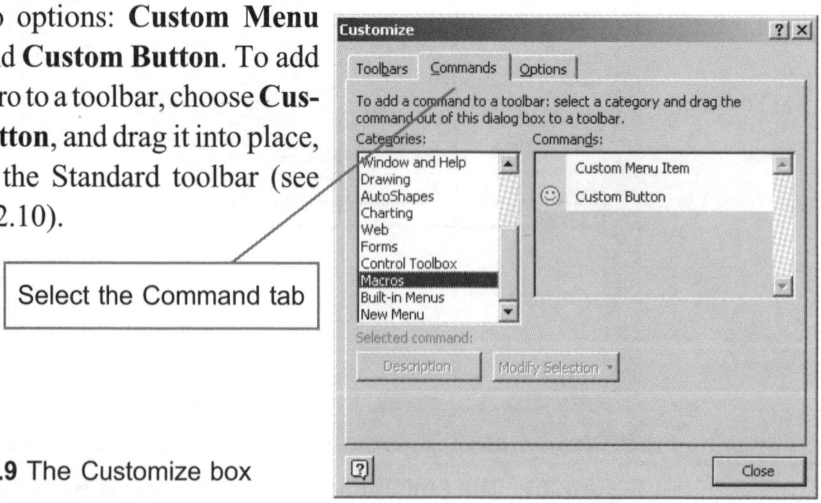

> Select the Command tab

Figure2.9 The Customize box

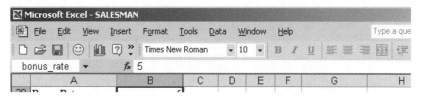

Figure 2.10 The custom button (smiley icon) added to the Standard toolbar, placed between the **Save** icon and the **Chart Wizard** icon.

4   To assign the custom button to a macro, highlight it and click the mouse. The **Assign Macro** dialog box (see Figure 2.11) will appear, from where you can assign a macro to the button.

Adding macros to a menu

To add a macro to a menu:

1   Select **View** > **Toolbars** > **Customise** to open the **Customise** dialog box.

2   Open the **Commands** page, and select **Macros** from the **Categories** list.

3   In the **Commands** list for macros, choose the **Custom Menu Item**. Click the menu to which you want to add the macro, and while it is visible, drag the **Custom Menu Item** and drop it to the desired position on the menu.

4   Click **Custom Menu Item** on the menu, and the **Assign Macro** dialog box will appear, from where you can select and assign a macro as we have seen earlier in this chapter.

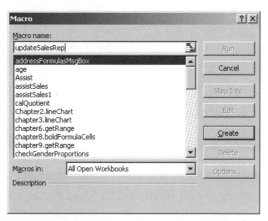

Figure 2.11 Attaching a macro

Macros for Excel charts

Charts are graphical representation of numeric data. Charts make it easier for users to compare and understand numbers – this is why they have become such a popular way of presenting numeric data. Charts can be created in Excel quite easily using the Chart Wizard, however, this is time-consuming, and macros can be automated and activated more quickly. Charts fall into two main categories:

* *Series charts*
* *Pie charts*.

Pie charts

Pie charts – so-called because they display data as segments in a circular pie shape – show the relationships between pieces of an entity. For example, we could produce a pie chart to show the breakdown in overall total sales over the last four weeks. Such a relationship would show the proportions of each of the weeks sales (see Figure 2.12). However, we would not be able to see any time trend from this type of diagram and for this situation, a series chart would be more appropriate.

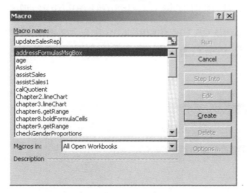

Figure 2.12 Illustration of pie chart

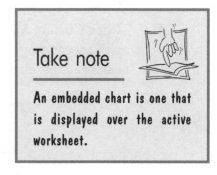

Take note

An embedded chart is one that is displayed over the active worksheet.

Series charts

The purpose of a series chart is to compare changes in some variable over time perhaps. The most widely used series charts are *line charts* and *area charts*. As the name suggests line charts display simple lines to depict changes, whereas, area charts displays areas filled below the lines. In all series charts, the horizontal line is called the x-axis and the vertical line is called the y-axis. Often x is known as the independent variable and y the dependent variable, i.e. y depends on x.

Suppose that we were interested in viewing the trend in the total sales for each week during the previous month in the *weeklysales* worksheet. We could create a series chart – called a line chart – as shown in Figure 2.17. The title of the chart is 'Total Weekly Sales for Month', and the total sales are plotted against the week number. We can record the macro for this task by the following steps:

1   Open the workbook called SALESMAN.XLS.

2   Select the worksheet *weeklysales*.

3   Choose **Tools > Macro > Record New Macro**. You will see the **Macro** dialog box appear – enter the name *'lineChart'*.

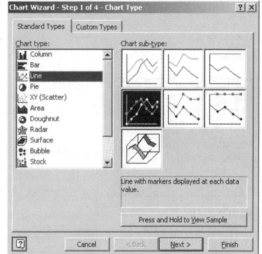

4   Select the range of cells from C41 to F41.

5   Click the **Chart Wizard** button on the Formatting toolbar – you will see the dialog box (Figure 2.13), select the Line chart type and click the **Next** button.

Figure2.13 Chart type selection

6   The dialog box shown in Figure 2.14 will appear. Make sure that **Rows** is selected and click the **Next** button.

7   The **Chart Options** dialog box will appear. You will need to enter the **Chart Title** as well as the **Category** (X) axis and the Y value name for the chart (see Figure 2.15). When done, click the **Next** button.

8   At the **Chart Location** dialog box (see Figure 2.16), make sure that the **AsObject** option is selected and click the **Finish** button.

9   You will now see the chart appear in the worksheet (see Figure 2.17).

10 Click the **Stop recording** macro button.

Figure 2.14 Select chart source data

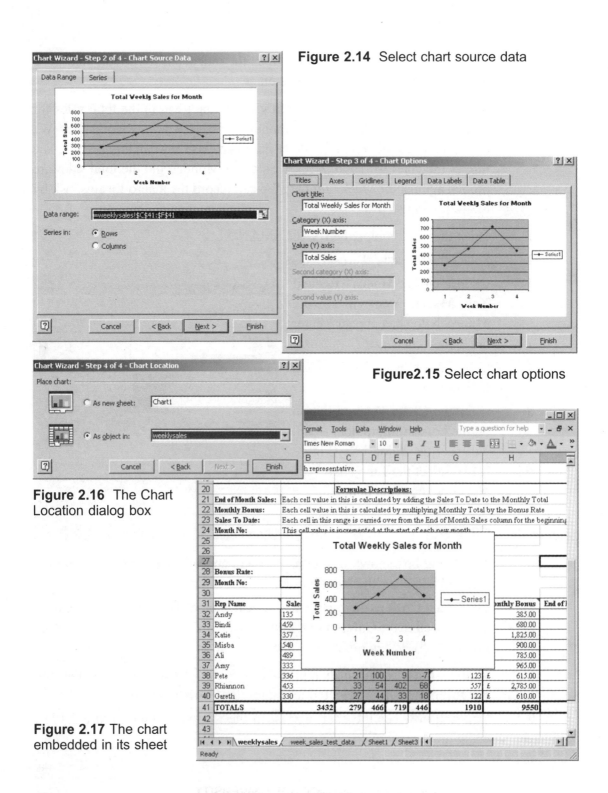

Figure2.15 Select chart options

Figure 2.16 The Chart Location dialog box

Figure 2.17 The chart embedded in its sheet

The Visual Basic toolbar

Excel contains a Visual Basic toolbar that groups actions for manipulating macros. To view this toolbar choose **View > Toolbars** and select **Visual Basic**. The toolbar (see Figure 2.18) include buttons for the following:

- **Run Macro** displays the Macros dialog box, in which any currently available macro can be selected to run.

- **Record Macro** displays the Record Macro dialog box. Note that when the Visual Basic toolbar is on screen, the Record Macro button appears depressed; clicking can stop the macro.

- **Security Button** displays the Security dialog box where you can select the security level. There are three levels from *high* – where macros are only accepted by the system from trusted sources, to protect against macro viruses, to *low* – with no protection. The default level is *medium*.

- **Visual Basic Editor** switches to the Visual Basic Editor – see Chapter 3.

- **Control Toolbox** toggles the display of the Control Toolbox toolbar. This lets you add controls such as buttons, edit boxes, and so on, to Excel worksheets.

- **Design Mode** switches the current document to Design mode; it also displays the Control Toolbox. The Design mode button is another toggle button (toggling between Exit Design and Design mode).

- **Microsoft Script Editor** activates an editor that enables the creation of HTML and XML pages.

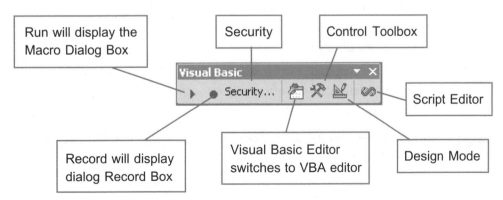

Figure2.18 The Visual Basic toolbar

Macro security issues

When you try to open a workbook in Excel that contains one or more macros, you will probably see the dialog box appear as shown in Figure 2.19. Its purpose is to alert the user that macros may contain viruses. This could be true if the macros are from an unknown, or external source. If you are confident the macros are safe, then you can click the **Enable Macros** button.

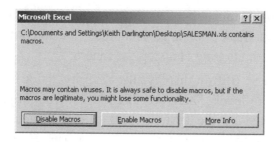

Figure 2.19 Enable Macro dialog box

Security levels

On more recent versions of Excel, such as XP, you will find that you can assign security levels for accepting macros when opening Excel files. This means that if a file includes a macro from a non-trusted source, then macros will be disabled. To assign a security choose: **Tools > Macro > Security...** from whence a dialog box will appear as shown in Figure 2.20. Notice that you can set three levels of security:

- *High* – only signed macros from trusted sources accepted, all other macros are disabled.

- *Medium* – user can choose whether to run potentially unsafe macros. This is the default level.

- *Low* – all macros accepted. Use only if you are confident all macros are safe, or unless you have macro anti-virus software installed.

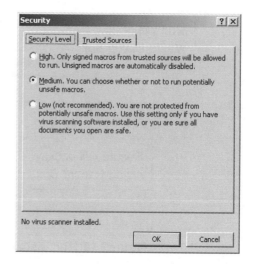

Figure 2.20 Setting security levels

Exercises

1   Open the file SALESMAN.XLS. Write a recorded macro to make all data in the *week_sales* range of the *weeklysales* worksheet bold face and place a border around the *week_sales* range. Link the macro to a button named *border* to be placed on the right-hand side of the worksheet.

2   Open the Excel workbook SALESMAN.XLS. Create a recorded macro called *print_main_data*, which will select the range from A31 to I41. The macro should then print this area by using: **File > Print Area > Set Print Area**. Test the macro.

3   Create a button called *Print Main Area* and place it on the *weeklysales* worksheet. Its purpose should be to allow users to highlight a range of cells on the spreadsheet before clicking the button. By clicking the button, users will obtain a printout of the selected range.

4   Write a recorded macro called *generate_random*. The macro should generate random numbers between 0 and 100 and place them in the selected test data range of the *week_sales_test_data* worksheet of the SALESMAN workbook. Hint: to place a random number in a cell between 0 and 800, you can use the built-in Excel function *Int(Rand()*801)*. This function works

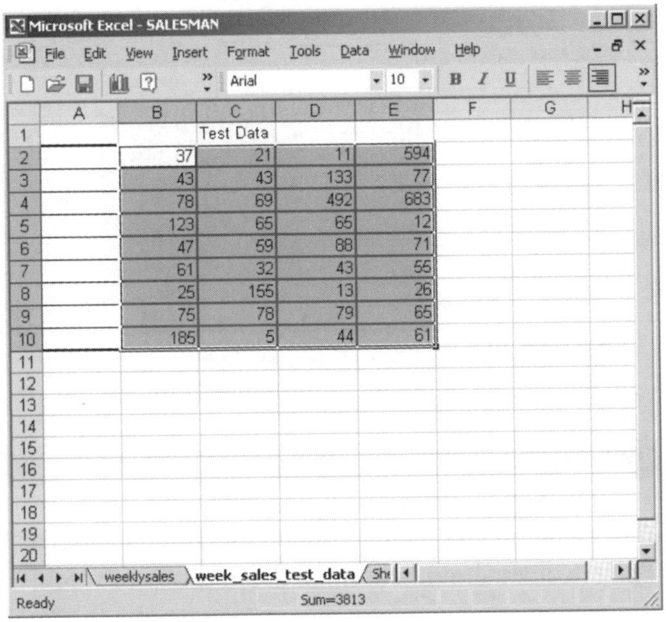

Figure 2.21 The *test_data* range in the *week_sales_test_data* sheet giving random numbers.

because *Rand ()* will generate a random number between 0 and 1. Hence, when multiplied by 801 it turns it into a decimal number between 0 and 800. The *Int()* function will truncate the part after the decimal point giving a value between 0 and 800.

5   Open the Excel workbook SALESMAN.XLS. Create a recorded macro called *copy_test_data*. Its purpose is to copy the selected data from the *test_data range* of the *week_sales_test_data* (see Figure 2.21), and paste this data into the named range *week_sales* of the (see Figure 2.22) *weeklysales* worksheet. Run and test the macro. Select **Tools > Macro > Macros** to see the **Macro** dialog box. Highlight the *copy_test_data* macro and choose **Edit** to view the VBA program. Briefly study the program – in the next chapter we will be writing programs in the VBA language.

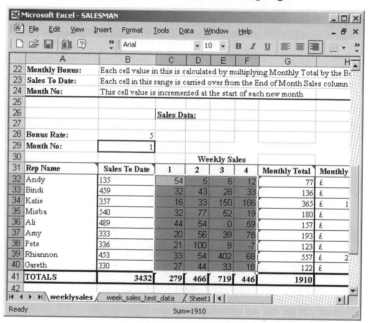

Figure 2.22 The selected range *week_sales* of the *weeklysales* worksheet

6   Write a recorded macro to create the 3-D pie chart as shown in Figure 2.12. The pie chart should chart the proportions of weekly sales during a month.

3 Introduction to VBA

Excel and VBA 44

The VBA environment 45

Structured English pseudocode . . . 50

Input and output in VBA 52

Running VBA modules 57

Tips for running VBA macros 59

Calculations in VBA 61

VBA for Excel Help 63

Creating and naming a module . . 65

Exercises 66

Excel and VBA

In the previous chapter, we looked at a quick and easy way to create a macro using the macro recorder. The macro records the Excel commands as instructions – code for the VBA language. However, recording a macro is not adequate for every Excel task. For example, consider the *updateSalesRep* recorded macro that we created in the previous chapter. Suppose it was required to increment the month number (*month_no* range) after the other parts of the macro have been completed? It would not be possible to perform this task as a recorded macro because any attempt to increment the *month_no* will trigger a circular reference to this cell. This is one example of an action that cannot be recorded: this task can only be completed by using the VBA programming language. These are other good reasons as we will see in the coming chapters.

Before we look at the VBA environment, we need to understand the relationship between Excel and VBA. An Excel application consists of two separate and interconnected environments: the workbook environment containing worksheets, charts, etc., and the VBA environment which contains the means to write programs that will interface with the workbook. Data and information can be passed from Excel to VBA and vice versa. As we can see from the diagram, the workbook environment contains the familiar worksheets and charts. The other part contains modules that contain the VBA macro code. Before we look at modules and VBA code, it is important to gain familiarity with the VBA development environment – also called the Visual Basic Editor (VBE).

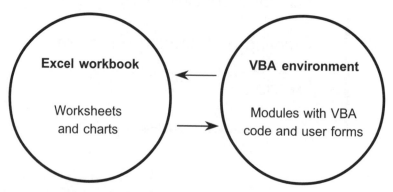

Figure 3.1 The relationship Between Excel and VBA

The VBA environment

To use the VBA environment (the VBE), first open a new workbook in Excel, then select: **Tools > Macro >Visual Basic Editor**. Alternatively, hit the keyboard combination **[Alt] + [F11]**. A window similar to that shown in Figure 3.2 will appear. This contains the title bar along with the Menu bar – a standard feature of all Windows applications – and the Standard toolbar.

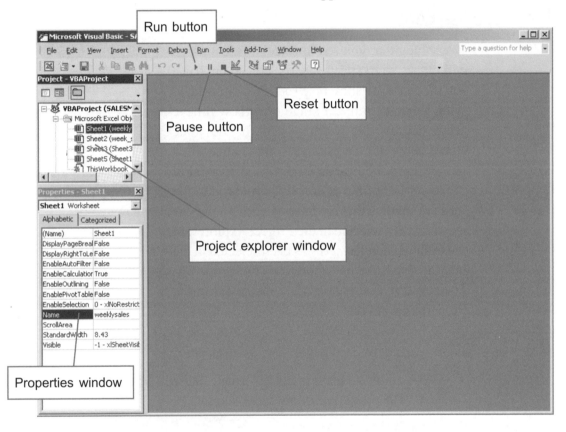

Figure 3.2 The VBA environment

Project Explorer

The main window contains a number of panes. The one in the top-left of the screen is called the Project Explorer. Its purpose is to enable the programmer to explore, using a tree structure, all open projects and their components.

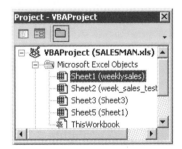

Project Explorer operates in a similar way to the Windows Explorer. A plus sign next to a folder indicates that the folder contains objects whose names are not displayed currently, a minus sign indicates the folder is fully open.

Note that objects will be studied in depth in the next chapter.

The Properties pane

Everything that you see in Excel/VBA, such as cell ranges, worksheets, charts, and so on, has a set of characteristics or *properties* associated with it. For example, a range of cells will have properties like the width of cells or the value stored in a cell. We can view and change these properties in the Properties pane – displayed in the lower left of the editor. Its purpose is to list those properties that are associated with the object currently selected in the Project Explorer. In the example here, *Sheet1* has been selected in the Project Explorer, and therefore, the properties associated with this object are displayed in the Properties window.

The VBA Editor

The VBA editor window is used to create and edit VBA program files. To create a VBA program, follow these steps:

1   Select **Tools>Macro>Macros...** to invoke the **Macro** dialog box as shown in Figure 3.3.

2   Type in a meaningful macro name, such as: UpdateSales and click the Create button. You will see the VBE screen appear as shown in Figure 3.4.

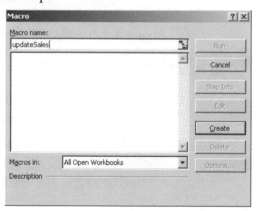

Figure 3.3 The Macro dialog box

Note that the larger pane on the right-hand side appear in the VBE. This is almost blank – apart from the inclusion of the Sub UpdateSales() and End Sub. This is the Editor window, and each window that is used is known as a module. A module is used to store the VBA program code.

Now type in the rest of the source code as shown in Listing 3.1. Be careful when entering the first two lines below the *Sub UpdateSales():* these are comment lines – text preceded by an apostrophe. Comments are ignored by the VBA program and are intended to help the programmer understand the code. They are coloured green in the VBA editor. You are free to insert as many comments as is required. Some tips for using comments in programs are given in the section on programming style (page 50).

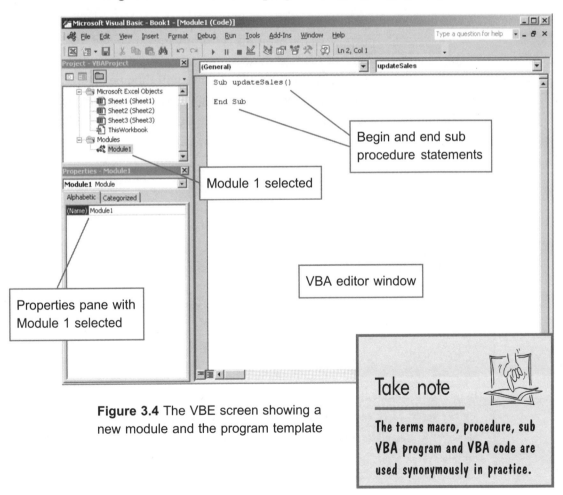

Figure 3.4 The VBE screen showing a new module and the program template

Take note

The terms macro, procedure, sub VBA program and VBA code are used synonymously in practice.

Listing 3.1 The sales update VBA macro

```
1    Sub updateSales()
2       'Update Sales VBA program Version 1.0
3
4       Worksheets("Weeklysales").  Select
5       ActiveSheet.Unprotect
6       Range("End_month_sales").Copy
7       Range("sales_to_date").PasteSpecial  xlValues
8       Range("Week_sales").ClearContents
9       Range ("month_no") = Range ("month_no") + 1
10      ActiveSheet.Protect
11   End Sub
```

> Do not include the line numbers in your code – they are here simply to identify the lines in the text.

This is a similar example to the recorded Excel macro *updateSalesRep* in Chapter 2. The purpose of the example is to copy the range *end_month_sales* and paste the values into the range *sales_to_date*. The *week_sales* range that contains the week sales data during the month will then be cleared ready to receive the data for the next month. Unlike the recorded version, we will also alter the cell named *month_no*, so that it will be increased by 1 at the end of each month.

The window that contains the code is called a *module*. A module is a separate file that contains a collection of one or more macros. You can store each macro in a separate module or save them all in the same one. As a general rule, it is advisable to store related macros in the same module. For example, if you have a number of calculation macros in your workbook, then they should be stored in the same module. This should make the macro easier to

Take note

In the Visual Basic Editor, the words Sub and End Sub are displayed in dark blue. These are key words, reserved by VBA as system commands. The update sales() part appears in black. VBA uses different colours for different types of statements. Statements, which contain syntax errors – lines that are grammatically incorrect – will appear in red.

find when required for editing. The macros in the module are available throughout the application.

You can also see that the beginning of the procedure named *UpdateSales*. Line 2 is a comment line. A comment begins with the ' symbol, or *Rem* (short for 'remark') and does not cause VBA to perform any action when the program is run. They are used to document programs and improve readability.

Line 3 is a blank line, inserted to enhance program readability (i.e. by separating the comments from the rest of the program statements). It's vital to learn to use proper program documentation style from the beginning.

Line 4 is the first command in the VBA program. It sets the active sheet to *weeklysales*, so that the correct sheet is manipulated by the macro.

The statement in line 5 will unprotect the worksheet so that changes can be made to it.

The statement in line 6 will copy the range *end_month_sales* into the Clipboard.

The statement in line 7 will then paste this range, by values, from the Clipboard to the range *sales_to_date*.

The statement in line 8 will clear the contents of the cell *range week_sales*.

The statement in line 9 will increment the contents of the *month_no* range.

The statement in line 10 will protect the sheet from inadvertent changes.

The statement in line 11 will end the program.

Take note

A macro is also known as a *procedure*. There are two types of procedures available in VBA. They are: sub procedures and function procedures. Function procedures will be studied in Chapter 9. Every sub procedure written in VBA must begin with a **Sub** keyword followed by the name of the procedure and opening and closing parenthesis as shown in Listing 3.1, Line 1. Every sub procedure must end with an **End Sub** statement (see Listing 3.1 Line 11).

Structured English pseudocode

Structured English is an informal language that helps the programmer to 'think out' the actual program steps before actually writing in a formal programming language such as VBA. Structured English is similar to everyday English and therefore is a useful step before translation to VBA code. It is not a programming language and its purpose is to aid code writing. This means that you don't need to be precise with structured English because it is not proper computer code. Also, include executable statements only when writing in structured English. The previous program that updates monthly sales is written in structured English as shown in Listing 3.2.

Listing 3.2 Structured English version of Listing 3.1

```
UpdateSales
    Unprotect the Weekly Sales sheet
    Select and Copy the End_month_sales range
    Select the sales_to_date range and
    Paste in the Value of the copied cells
    Clear the Contents of the Week_sales range
    Increment month_no
    Protect the Weekly Sales sheet
End pseudocode
```

Programming style

Many students who are new to computer programming assume that getting the program to work correctly is all that matters! However, even when a program is working correctly, changes to the program might be necessary in the future. Research has shown that program maintenance accounts for over 67per cent of software development time. There are many reasons why maintenance becomes necessary. For example, it may be necessary to make changes to the functionality of a program, or perhaps the organisation that the program was written for has changed their procedures in some way. Improving the layout and readability of the program will make maintenance easier. Both can be achieved by following these style guidelines:

♦   Ensure that VBA program code contains enough comments. Comments should typically be placed at the start of a VBA program, such as details that include the date the program was written, the program version number, the name of the programmer, and any other things that might help with understanding the code. Other comments might be included to the right of a VBA statement. It is also good programming practice to leave some spaces before in-line comments begin to improve readability.

- Use blank lines to separate distinct sections in a program to enhance the readability of the code. For example, the blank line in line 3 of Listing 3.1 separates the comments from the beginning of the main body of code.

- Indent VBA program statements inside the body of the macro name and any other VBA statement blocks. It is recommended that the number of characters for indentation be no less than three spaces. Indenting is not essential. Your programs will work without it, but it does make it easier to identify errors. Note that it is better to use the Tab key on the keyboard for indenting lines; otherwise if you use the Space Bar you will probably end up with inconsistent indenting.

- As a general rule, you should indent the main program block, i.e., between the **Sub...** and **End Sub** lines. You should also indent any other blocks of code within these lines. Examples of blocks are: **If...End If**, or **With...End With**.

- Use a consistent naming convention for items used in VBA program design (more on this in Chapter 5). Meaningful names should be assigned to items, saying something about the item being named.

- Use meaningful names for VBA macros. These will help you to know which one to choose in the **Select macro** list of the **Macro** dialog box. I have used names for Sub procedures such that they use alphabetic characters only and use capital letters for the second and later words. For example, if we were naming a procedure to name print a character, then the sub procedure would be named *printCharacter*.

Self-assessment exercise

View the recorded VBA code for the macro *UpdateSalesRep* that you created in Chapter 2. To do this, use **Tools > Macro** then select the macro in the dialog box and click the **Edit** button. Study the code carefully and compare it with VBA code from the procedure written in Listing 3.1. What are the main differences in the two programs?

Input and output in VBA

Most programming languages will contain commands that enable the user to input data from the keyboard and output results on the monitor display. Of course, data could be input and displayed by using worksheet cells in Excel. However, this may not be appropriate for it might be necessary to input or output without using worksheet cells. A function is defined as something in VBA/Excel that will return a value and will be familiar to any Excel user. Functions will be studied in more detail in Chapter 9. VBA for Excel supports two built-in functions for the primary purpose of input and output. They are **InputBox** and **MsgBox.**

The InputBox function

The **InputBox** function enables a user to input data through a dialog box (see Figure 3.5). Notice that the generic dialog box has two buttons: **OK** (the default selection) and **Cancel**. These buttons can be customised (see Chapter 10). The dialog box also contains a title (in this case "Ask Age"), a prompt ("How old are you?") and a text box for the user's input. The **InputBox** function takes at least one parameter: a prompt to the user. The format for using this function in a VBA program is illustrated in the following example:

```
strAge = InputBox("How old are you?", "Ask Age")
```

Here, the prompt to the user is the message "How old are you?" The title of the dialog box is "Ask Age" and this is given from the second parameter in the **InputBox** function. When this command is run in VBA, the cursor will flash in the edit line while waiting for the user to respond with some data. In Figure 3.5, the value 48 has been entered; this value will now be stored in a place called *strAge*. This is known as a *variable* because any value could have been entered in the text box; i.e., it could vary. Variables are studied in detail in Chapter 5.

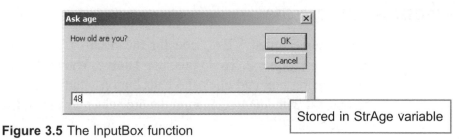

Figure 3.5 The InputBox function

Self-assessment exercise

Write the VBA statement that will display an input box containing the title: "Ask Children" with the prompt: "How many children do you have?"

The MsgBox function

The purpose of the **MsgBox** function is to display results. A simple example of output using it is illustrated in Figure 3.6. Notice that a generic MsgBox contains only an **OK** button. A title – the default being Microsoft Excel in the absence of the programmer supplying one – and some output contained in the MsgBox (in this case the message: 'Hello!').

The VBA statement:

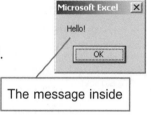

The message inside

    MsgBox "Hello!"

Would produce the output as shown in Figure 3.6.

Figure 3.6 The MsgBox Function

MsgBox customisation

A **MsgBox** function can be customised in many ways, as the example in Figure 3.7 shows. A number of examples follow that illustrate customisation. The first example provides a meaningful title "To whom it may concern" in the Title bar by replacing the default "Microsoft Excel" title. This example also uses an indicator inside the dialog box of the type of data being displayed – in this case "i" for information. This variation is produced by including two optional arguments in the **MsgBox** statment as follows and produces the output shown in 3.7:

    MsgBox "Hello!", vbInformation, "To whom it may concern"

The information icon — Hello! — Displays this title in Titlebar

Figure 3.7 The MsgBox function including title display

Using MsgBox with Yes or No Buttons

MsgBox has other uses apart from output display. For instance, a MsgBox could be used to get the user to make a simple choice of two or more options, and then take appropriate program action depending on the choice made. If the programmer were to customise the layout of the MsgBox to include two buttons taking values **Yes**, or **No**, then the statement:

```
Outcome = MsgBox ("Do you like Bananas?", vbYesNo, "Tastes in fruit
question")
```

would have the effect of producing the output as shown in Figure 3.8. Note how the parenthesis has been placed around the right-hand side following the **MsgBox** keyword. This is required if you wish to capture the result of the choice given in the message box. In the above example we have captured the result of the MsgBox in the variable *Outcome*. More will be said about variables in Chapter 5 – all you need to know at this stage is that in the above statement the variable Outcome will store a value, when the user chooses a response from either **Yes** or **No** in the message box. It will not actually store 'Yes' or 'No', but instead it will hold coded values as shown in Table 3.2. For example, suppose we wanted to write VBA code that would prompt the user with the MsgBox as shown in Figure 3.8, and respond with a message box stating "Good Taste!" if the user replied with the answer **Yes**. This would be implemented with the following fragment of VBA code:

```
Outcome = MsgBox ("Do you like Bananas?", vbYesNo, "Tastes in
    fruit question")
If (Outcome =6 ) Then
    MsgBox "Good Taste!"
End If
```

The statement **If (Outcome =6) Then** checks to see if the value assigned to the variable *Outcome* is equal to 6, which – as can be seen from Table 3.2 – means choosing the option **Yes**. If this statement is true, then the MsgBox "Good Taste!" is executed, otherwise it is not. The statement **End If** terminates the **If** block. (See Chapter 6 for more on the **If** statement.)

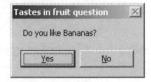

Figure 3.8 The MsgBox function using Yes/No choices

Self assessment exercise

Write the VBA statement that will display a message box that contains the title: "Play Tennis" with the prompt: "Do you play tennis?" and two buttons taking **Yes** or **No** values.

Using MsgBox with Yes, No and Cancel buttons

A number of other button combinations can be used with MsgBox. These include displaying **Yes**, **No** and **Cancel** buttons. The following VBA statement will implement this:

```
answer = MsgBox (Title:="Confirm Choice ", Prompt: ="Do you want to
save this file?", Buttons: = 3)
```

The effect of this statement will produce the output shown below:

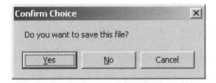

Figure 3.9 The MsgBox function with Yes /No and Cancel buttons

In the example shown in Figure3.9, **Title**, **Prompt**, and **Buttons** have been assigned values. The Title and Prompt text values are, as expected, displayed in the appropriate **MsgBox** positions. The Buttons assignment takes any value in the range 1 to 6 and generates a different combination of buttons depending on the value chosen (see Table 3.1).

Table 3.1 MsgBox buttons options

Value	Response Buttons displayed		
1	OK	Cancel	
2	Abort	Retry	Ignore
3	Yes	No	Cancel
4	Yes	No	
5	Retry	Cancel	
6	OK		

Table 3.2 MsgBox return values

Value Returned	Constant	Description
1	vbOK	The OK button has been pressed
2	vbCancel	The Cancel button has been pressed
3	vbAbort	The Abort button has been pressed
4	vbRetry	The Retry button has been pressed
5	vbIgnore	The Ignore button has been pressed
6	vbYes	The Yes button has been pressed
7	vbNo	The No button has been pressed

General syntax of MsgBox function

The examples given above on the use of the **MsgBox** function by no means describe all possible variations on the way that it can be used. However, the general syntax takes the following form:

MsgBox *(Prompt [, Buttons] [, Title])*

Where *Prompt* contains the text to be displayed in the dialog box.

♦ Buttons determine the number and types of buttons to be displayed

♦ Title contains the text to be displayed in the title bar of the message box.

Forcing a line break in a message box

To force a line break in a message box, you can use the **vbCrLf** constant as shown in the following example code.

```
Sub newLineProg()
 MsgBox "Three blind mice." & vbCrLf & "See how they run."
End Sub
```

Figure3.10 Line breaks in a MsgBox

Take note

You can use the &vbCrLf (carriage return Line feed) constant with Excel 97 or later. With Excel 95, use the ASCII codes for the Carriage Return Chr(13) and the Linefeed Chr(10) — see Appendix 1.

Running VBA modules

An Excel/VBA application can be anything from a small routine that performs a useful service to a large application that completely shields the user from Excel's basic interface. Excel provides a variety of ways to launch an application that can be tailored to suit the system. The ways is which an Excel VBA program can be launched are as follows:

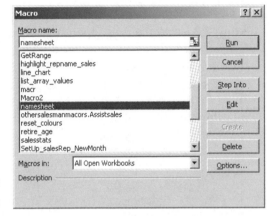

+ By using **Tools > Macro > Macros**, selecting the macro and clicking the Run button (see Figure 3.11).

    Figure 3.11 Invoking a macro with the Macro dialog box.

+ By assigning a button to the macro. Examples of this were given in Chapter 2.

+ By assigning your VBA procedure to a built-in macro. Excel contains four built-in automatic macros, which are invoked when some event occurs. These built-in macros are:

    Auto_Open – invoked whenever a workbook containing the macro is opened.

    Auto_Close – invoked whenever the workbook containing the macro is closed.

    OnSheetActivate – invoked when you first enter data on a worksheet.

    OnEntry – invoked when you enter a worksheet.

Using Auto_Open

The following example illustrates how the **Auto_Open** procedure can be used to provide a start up message. The example shown in Listing 3.1 will give a different message for each day of the week. On Monday the message given is "Have a nice week", on Tuesday the message is "One down, four to go!", and so on. The procedure works by creating a variable that will contain the digits from 1 to 7 representing the days of the week. It then finds out what day it is, using a built-in function that returns the current day (more on this in Chapter 9), and a **Case** statement to decide what to do for each day of the week (more on this in Chapter 9). Don't worry about your understanding of this just yet, as long as you can see how **Auto-Open()** works. The line **select Case dayNum** is used to choose the current day and to associate the appropriate message so that it can then be output in a message box.

Listing 3.3 Using the Auto_open macro

```
Sub Auto_Open ()
'Example auto open macro to give a day of the week message
Dim dayNum As Integer
dayNum = Weekday(Date)
Select Case dayNum
    Case 2: MsgBox "Today is Monday!"
    Case 3: MsgBox "Today is Tuesday!"
    Case 4: MsgBox "Today is Wednesday!"
    Case 5: MsgBox "Today is Thursday!"
    Case 6: MsgBox "Today is Friday!"
    Case Else: MsgBox "Happy Weekend!"
End Select
End Sub
```

Note how the Case statements are indented between the Select Case dayNum and End Select block.

Figure 3.12 Sample MsgBox from Listing 3.1

Take note

The built-in macros Auto_Open, Auto_Close, etc., have been replaced by *event procedures* (see Chapter 10) in Excel 97 and above, but they are still supported for compatibility with workbooks created in previous versions. It is recommended that you do not to use the Auto_Open and Auto_Close macros in new workbooks. For even though they do what is required, implementing *event procedures* is more appropriate now (see Chapter 10). They have been included here for two reasons. If you are developing a workbook that will make use of versions of Excel before 97, you must use the Auto_Open and Auto_Close macros. Moreover, you might still see them being used by other programmers.

Tips for running VBA macros

The following tips may help relieve stress when running VBA procedures:

- Always include the statement: **Activesheet.Unprotect** before the main body of program instructions begin. This enables changes to be made to the active worksheet. If you fail to do this, then you will probably get a runtime error in your program. You can always re-protect the sheet when the macro is complete.

- Always ensure that the correct worksheet is selected by including an statement of the form: **Worksheets ("*mySheet*").Select** before the program instructions begin, where *mySheet* is the worksheet that is required to be the active sheet during the running of the macro. If you fail to do this and some other worksheet is active during the program run, then the macro instructions might be applied to the wrong worksheet with unpredictable and, possible very undesirable consequences.

- Make sure that any named ranges that are referred to in a VBA macro exist, and are correctly spelt. This is a common source of errors, and can be avoided by checking the names of each of the named ranges by using the Excel named range box. Click the **Name** box at the left-hand end of the formula bar in Excel to see what Name ranges exist in your workbook.

- Don't try to run a macro until it is ready. If your macro refuses to run, check for obvious obstructions, i.e., make sure that you have no dialog box awaiting a response, or that you are not currently editing a cell in the worksheet that you are using, and so on.

- If you are typing a VBA statement that is excessively long, you can continue from one statement to the other by using the underscore (_) character. To use this, first type a space at the point where you want to finish the line, and then type the underscore character, and then continue the typing on the next line. Remember, you must have the space before, and after, the underscore character.

- If you want to temporarily remove a statement in a VBA program, you can comment out the statement by inserting the comment symbol (') before the statement line begins. This circumvents the need for re-typing the line again when it is to be used.

The improved UpdateSales macro

If we go back to the *UpdateSales* macro earlier in this chapter, you will recall that among other things, the *month_no* was incremented ready for the next month before ending the macro. The problem with the macro however, is that if it is used every month, then eventually it will contain the value 13, and this of course does not make sense as there are 12 months in a year. For this reason, this example will extend that macro so that whenever the *month_no* value exceeds 12, it is reset to 1. We can use the VBA **If… Then** statement to do this as can be seen on line 11. This checks to see **If** a condition is met – in this case **month_no >12** – and if it is, **Then** the statement(s) will be executed. That is, the *month_no* value is reset to 1.

The full code is shown in Listing 3. 4. Notice the lines 11 to 13 have been included to implement this part. **If Range("month_no") >12 Then** checks to see if the *month_no* is greater than 12, and if it is the action in line 12 is taken, i.e. **Range ("month_no") = 1**. Line 13 will end the **If** block: this means the actions following the true condition are complete.

Note how the statements are indented between **If Range ("month_no") >12 Then** and **End If**.

Listing 3.4 The UpdateSales macro updated to include decision

```
1    Sub Updatesales ()
2        'Update Sales VBA program Version 1.0
3        'Written by Keith Darlington Date 12/1/03
4
5        Worksheets ("Weeklysales").select
6        ActiveSheet.Unprotect
7        Range ("End_month_sales").Copy
8        Range ("sales_to_date").PasteSpecial xlValues
9         Range ("Week_sales").ClearContents
10       Range ("month_no") = Range ("month_no") + 1
11       If Range (month_no"> 12 Then
12           Range ("month_no") =1
13       End If
14       ActiveSheet.Protect
15   End Sub
```

> If the *month_no* is greater than 12, *month_no* is set to 1

Calculations in VBA

Some of the examples looked at to date have involved mathematical calculations. Many of the symbols that are used in everyday arithmetic are the same in VBA programs. For example, the (+) sign for addition and the (-) minus sign for subtraction. However, because of keyboard ambiguities and difficulties, there are some arithmetical symbols that are different. For instance, the arithmetical multiplication symbol (×) is denoted by the asterisk symbol (*) on a computer. The reason for not using the x symbol is to prevent ambiguity with the alphabetical meaning of x. Also, exponentiation is denoted by a superscript in everyday arithmetic, but this is difficult to implement on a computer keyboard and therefore the symbol for exponentiation is the caret (^).

Table 3.3 displays the VBA arithmetic operators and their everyday equivalents. Note the two additional operators that are available in VBA programs, namely integer division (\) and modulo division (Mod).

- When integer division is used, the integer portion of the result is returned only, e.g. **9 \ 2 = 4** (the fractional part of the quotient is discarded).
- When modulo division is used, the integer portion of the result is discarded and the remainder is returned, e.g. **9 Mod 2 =1** since the remainder part is 1.

Operator	Math symbol	VBA symbol	Math example	VBA example
Addition	+	+	6+7	6+7
Subtraction	-	-	7-4	7-4
Multiplication	×	*	7x4	7*4
Division	÷	/	7÷4	7/4
Exponentiation		^	7^4	7^4
Integer division		\		7\2 (=3)
Modulo division		Mod		7 Mod 2 (= 1)

Table 3.3 VBA mathematical operators

Operator precedence

Arithmetical operators in VBA, as in everyday arithmetic, are not evaluated from left to right, but follow rules of precedence. These prevent ambiguity regarding the order in which arithmetical operations are to be followed. These rules of precedence can be memorised from the BODMAS mnemonic (Brackets, power Of, Division, Multiplication, Addition, Subtraction).

For instance, the expression 9 * 4 - 3 would give the result = 33, since multiplication (*) has a higher precedence than subtraction (-). Thus, 9 * 4 would be evaluated first giving 36, followed by 36 - 3 giving 33. On the other hand, the expression 9 * (4 - 3) would give the result = 9, as brackets have a higher precedence than multiplication. Thus, here the (4 - 3) part is evaluated first, giving 1 followed by multiplication by 9.

VBA for Excel Help

VBA contains a large number of built-in Help files which can be very useful both as a learning tool and a reference for information. Help can be invoked by using the **Help** option from the VBE, or by invoking the Help Assistant (the **[F1]** key). The **Help** dialog box, will appear (see Figure 3.13). The structure and layout of VBA Help is similar to help provided by other Windows applications in that it contains: **Contents**, **Answer Wizard** and **Index** tabs.

Figure 3.13 The VBA Help Contents Display

The *Contents* tab gives an on-line user manual type structure. When first selected a table of contents is displayed and you can click and move down to the section of interest. The *Answer Wizard* tab lets you enter a phrase and provide a topic list which you can choose from. The *Index* tab is used when you have a keyword name and wish to find further information. Again a list is provided of relevant topics. A sample Help screen is shown in Figure 3.14. Many concepts contain examples of their use. You are strongly advised to get familiar with the VBA Help system for it could prove to be very useful as you acquire VBA programming skills.

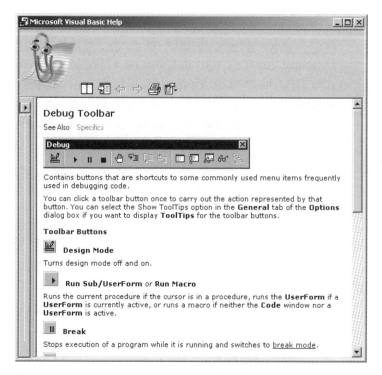

Figure 3.14 A sample Help screen from the VBE

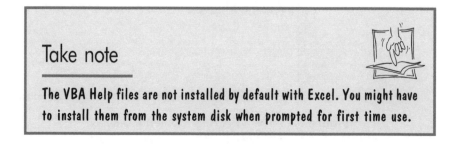

Take note

The VBA Help files are not installed by default with Excel. You might have to install them from the system disk when prompted for first time use.

Creating and naming a module

We saw earlier in this chapter that macros are stored in modules. Modules that are created by the VBA system are – like macros – given default names. These are *Module1*, *Module2* and so on. You can create a new module for writing a macro, by selecting the **Insert > Module** menu item from the VBE. You can also assign more meaningful names to modules as follows:

1   From the VBE, highlight the module that you want to name in the Project Explorer window.

2   In the Properties window click the **Name** item (see Figure 3.15), enter the name that you want to assign to the module and press the **[Enter]** key. You will see the module has been renamed with your choice in the Project Explorer window.

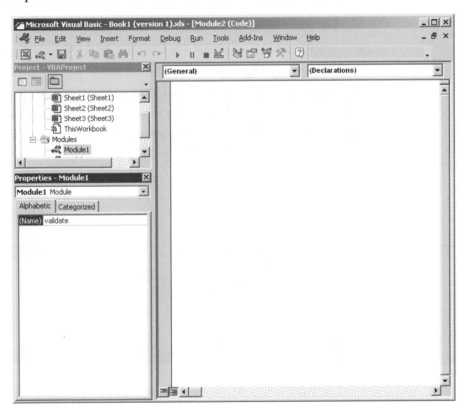

Figure 3.15 Changing the name of a module

Exercises

1   Copy the SALESMAN.XLS worksheet from the Website. The *weeklysales* worksheet is protected apart from the Week Sales input area. Perform the following tasks. Create a new macro using **Tools** > **Macro** > **Macros....** Enter the procedure as shown on Listing 3.4 (page 60). Make sure that the code is written exactly as shown, otherwise you will get error messages. Now do the following:

    a)   Run the procedure from the VBA editor by clicking the **Run** button on the Standard toolbar. Check the program works correctly by choosing: **File** > **Close and Return** to Microsoft Excel, alternatively, you can click the Excel icon on the Windows Taskbar.

    b)   Run the program from the *weeklysales* worksheet (you might like to input some test data into the *week_sales* named range because it will be empty if the procedure worked correctly from part (a).

    c)   Create a button on the *weeklysales* worksheet and assign the name *Updatesales* to it. Click on the button to run the procedure.

2   Design, using structured English pseudocode, a VBA sub procedure that will prompt the user to input a number representing a person's salary and then respond with a message box containing the message "Thank you". Now write the VBA code from the design.

3   Open a new workbook. Using the default *Sheet1*, enter the following macro using the VBE:

```
Sub ifGreaterThanTen()

    theAge = InputBox("Please input a number representing an adult age")
    If theAge < 18 Then
        MsgBox "Invalid data. An Adult is over 18"
    End If
End Sub
```

Explain what you think this program may be doing. Run the macro and check, using the data given to see that it works properly.

4 Introduction to objects

Object-oriented programming 68

Object collections 71

The Excel object model 75

The Object Browser 77

Referencing named ranges 84

Exercises 89

Object-oriented programming

In the real world, we use objects like televisions, mobile phones, compact disks and books everyday. In the same way, Excel and VBA uses objects – albeit non-physical in nature. If we think, for example, about a television set: the television has characteristics or *properties* associated with it, such as the size, the make, model, weight and colour. You can also do things to control the behaviour of this object, such as turn it on or off, adjust the volume, adjust the colour contrast or kick it (if it is annoying you that much). In VBA, we can refer to Excel/VBA objects in much the same way: that is, objects have properties associated with them and have things that can be done to them. The latter are called methods. In the case of Excel/VBA, the objects could be things like workbooks, worksheets, charts and cell ranges. We will look at properties and methods for these Excel/ VBA objects in the next sections. Those described in the next sections are not complete by any means.

Some properties of objects

As stated earlier, a property is a characteristic of an object – or a way of describing some aspect of it. When we try to describe the TV set we usually refer to its dimensions, colour, make, model, and so on. Moreover, these properties will have *values* associated with them, such as the size is a 28" screen, or the make might be a Sony television. In a similar way, when we describe properties of Excel objects, such as a range of cells, then properties of this object would be things like the name of the cell range, the cell width, and so on. A *Range* object in Excel is defined as a row, column, combination of rows and/or columns, a selection of many – not necessarily contiguous – cells, or even one cell.

Another example of an Excel object is a *Workbook*, and this would have properties such as the workbook name (there must be a name since it is a synonym for an Excel file), or password (i.e. a property that gives password access to the workbook). You can see from these examples that the properties of objects will differ, although there may be some in common. Each occurrence of each object has its own properties which you can look at and change. We will see how to do this later in this chapter. Examples of other properties typical VBA /Excel objects are given in Table 4.1.

Table 4.1 Summary of object properties and methods

Object	Some properties and typical values	Some methods
Range	*Name* identifies the range, for example *sales_to_date* *Column* lets the user know the number of the first column in the Range object *Formula* shows the user the formula in a Range object	*Select* selects a worksheet range to work with in some way *ClearContents* clears data from a range of selected cells. *Copy, Cut* and *Paste* are more examples of range methods
Worksheet	*Name* identifies the worksheet. For example, *Weeklysales* *Visible* indicates whether the worksheet is visible (i.e. active) – possible values are true or false (Boolean values)	*Select* selects the worksheet object *Delete* deletes a worksheet from the currently open workbook *Protect* protects the active sheet from any changes.
Workbook	*Name* identifies the workbook, for example SALESMAN.XLS *ReadOnly* – if true, the workbook is read only; if false, changes can be made to it *File format* – format of the file, e.g. .xls, xla *Password* – true if password protected.	*Save* used with this object, can be in the form Save or SaveAs: *Save* requires no arguments, *SaveAs* takes arguments such as FileName to use, *Open* takes the argument FileName
Chart	*Name* identifies the chart, for example *myChart*. *ChartType* – the chart type, e.g. pie, bar *HasLegend* makes the legend of a chart visible if set to true.	*Location* – a chart can be embedded in a worksheet or placed on a separate chart sheet *PlotArea* refers to the colour of the plot area of a chart.

Excel methods

A *method* is an action that can be performed with an object. For example, controlling the volume on a television set is a method that can be performed with a real-world object. The behaviour of any object can be controlled by using its methods. If we consider the Range object, you can do things to this object such as *Select* it to work with in some way, or you can *ClearContents* (deleting the cells in the range). You can also *Copy* the contents to the Clipboard, and so on. If we consider another object such as a worksheet, again, you could *Select* it to work with it, and you could also *Delete* it –

removing it from the currently open workbook, *Protect* it – i.e. prevent changes being made to it. Thus, methods, like properties, will differ from object to object, though objects of the same type will clearly share methods.

Self-assessment exercise

Give three examples of properties and methods of a motor car object.

Referencing an object's properties and methods

We reference the properties and methods of an object by using the dot notation (.), it is written in the following notation:

Object.Identifier

Where *Object* is a reference to an object, such as Range or Workbook, and *Identifier* could be a valid property or method, such as *Name* or *ClearContents*.

Examples

Range ("my_cells").ClearContents

is a reference to the *ClearContents* method of the Range object *my_cells*.

Worksheets("that_sheet").Range ("C1").value = 6.

In this example, property value 6 has been set in the cell range C1, in the worksheet called *that_sheet* of the Worksheets collection (see next section). Note that in this example, the worksheet reference has been included. When you need to refer to a specific worksheet, you have to include the worksheet reference. Otherwise, the active worksheet reference would be taken.

Charts ("Chart1").PlotArea.Interior.ColorIndex = 3.

In this example, the colour of the *PlotArea* of *chart1* of the charts collection (see next section) has been set to red (ColorIndex = 3).

Events

An event is something that can happen to an object. For example, clicking a button in a dialog box is an event. When a button is clicked, some action will follow, such as executing a macro. VBA for Excel is an event-driven language. We will be returning to event-driven programming later on.

Object collections

When we talk about real-world objects such as a television set, we think of a particular object, but it is just one of a collection of many others (a very large number in the entire world). This collection of objects is not the same thing as an individual object in the collection but it can be regarded as an object in its own right.

In the same way, we can talk about an object collection when dealing with Excel/VBA objects. We can define a collection as a group of related objects. Like other objects, collections have methods and properties associated with them. The most commonly used collection property is **Count**, whilst the most commonly used method is **Add**. As the name suggests, **Count** is used to count the number of objects in a collection; while the **Add** method is used to add a new object to a collection.

Referencing objects in an object collection

You might have noticed that when we referred to objects in the previous section, we sometimes used singular references to objects and sometimes plural references. For example, consider the reference to the object **Worksheets ("***that_sheet***")**. The **Worksheets** part is written in plural form and therefore is a collection. Any of these Worksheets is a Worksheet singular object. However, the part in parentheses **("***that_sheet***")** refers to a single worksheet in the collection whose name is *that_sheet*. This is how we reference single objects in a collection. Most Excel objects conform to this characterisation apart from the **Range** object. This is because a Range collection does not have a homogenous form. A range can be anything from a single cell to a column, a row, a rectangular group of cells, or even a union of a set of non-contiguous cells. For this reason we cannot refer to a Ranges collection. However, we can still refer to a range in a worksheet in a workbook as the following example shows:

```
Workbooks ("Salesman"). _
Worksheets ("Weeklysales").Range ("month_no")
```

This example references the *month_no* range of cells, of the *Weeklysales* worksheet, of the SALESMAN workbook.

Why reference object properties and methods?

There are many reasons why you would need to access object properties and methods within a VBA macro. They are:

First, it may be necessary to examine the current condition or status of an object by retrieving the value stored in a particular property. For example, you might want to examine the contents of a cell to decide on some action. In both of the following examples, if the outcome of some condition is true then a message will be displayed.

```
If ActiveCell.Value < 0 Then MsgBox "The active cell contains a
    negative value"
If Workbooks ("my_work").open =false then MsgBox "File named
    my_work does not exist"
```

Second, you might want to change the status of an object by setting the value stored in a particular property. For example:

```
Activecell.Value = 4                    'Set the value of the ActiveCell to 4

Range ("mortgage_no").Formula = "=$A$1+$A$2"
'Set a formula in the range called mortgage number to A1 + A2

ActiveSheet.Name = "WeekSales"
'Set the ActiveSheet name to WeekSales

ActiveWorkbook.WorkSheets ("WeekSales").Range ("month_no").value =1
'Set the value of the month number range of the WeekSales worksheet
 ' in the active workbook to 1

Charts ("Chart1").Name = myChart
'Set the chart called chart1 to the name myChart.

Range ("d1").Formula= "=2+a2"      'Set a formula in range d1 to 2+a2
```

Third, you might want to use a methods to cause the object to carry out one of its built-in tasks. For example, you might want to use the *Protect* method to protect a worksheet from being altered. Examples using an object method to carry out a built-in task would include things like:

```
Worksheet ("Sheet1").Select   'Selecting the worksheet called sheet1

Worksheet ("Sheet1").Protect 'Protecting the worksheet called sheet1

Range ("$B$2:$B$6").Copy
'Copying the cell range $B$2:$B$6 by Absolute reference

Range ("$A$2:$A$6").Paste
'Paste the cell range $A$2:$A$6 by Absolute reference
```

```
MsgBox ActiveCell.Address
'Display the cell address of the ActiveCell in a MsgBox

Set newSheet = ActiveWorkbook.Worksheets.Add
'Adds a new worksheet to the worksheets collection called newSheet
```

Some methods require arguments to clarify any possible ambiguity of intentions. For example, the *UpdateSales* macro in Chapter 2 included a statement in the macro which read:

```
Range ("sales_to_date"). PasteSpecial xlValues
```

This is an example of an object reference which includes the argument *xlValues*. Other possible arguments here could be *xlFormats* and *xlFormulas*. The purpose of using an argument is to enable Excel to know how to paste the range; whether it be pasting the values or the cell format, or the formulas. The notation used for referencing arguments is as follows:

```
Object.Method  Argument1, Argument2, ......
```

Examples

```
Range ("D1:D4").PasteSpecial xlFormats
'Pastes the cell formats only into the range D1 to D4.

ActiveCell.BorderAround Weight: =xlMedium
'Sets a medium weight border around the ActiveCell
```

Look at each of the statements in the example below. We can see that each line contains object references. We will identify the objects being used with their properties and methods. This program – and all future programs – has been stripped of comments for convenience. Nevertheless, you should make sure that all macros you write include plenty of comments.

Listing 4.1

```
1  Sub UpdateSales ()
2  ActiveSheet.Unprotect
3     Range ("End_month_sales").Copy
4     Range ("sales_to_date").PasteSpecial xlValues
5     Range ("Week_sales").ClearContents
6     Range ("month_no") = Range ("month_no") + 1
7     ActiveSheet.Protect
8  End Sub
```

> You first saw this as Listing 3.4.

Lines 1 and 8 are the procedure begin and end statements and so no object references are made in these statements.

Line 2 is a reference to the **Unprotect** method of the **ActiveSheet** object.

Line 3 references the **Copy** method of the **Range** object called *End_month_sales*.

Line 4 references the **Paste** method to paste the values of the **Range** object called *sales_to_date* by values as given in the **xlValues** argument.

Line 5 references the **ClearContents** method of the *Week_sales* object.

Line 6 increments the *month_no* range by 1 (Notice that the value property is implicit in this reference).

Finally, line 7 references the active worksheet method **Protect**.

Self-assessment exercise

Write a VBA statement that sets the value in the ActiveCell of the worksheet called *thisSheet* in the workbook called *thisBook* to the value 20.

The Excel object model

Many real-world objects can contain objects that are themselves objects. For example, the hardware of a computer system contains parts such as a monitor, speakers, keyboard, mouse, and so on. These are themselves objects – sometimes collections and individual – that have properties and methods associated with them. The same analogy can be made for example, when VBA for Excel interfaces with objects such as workbooks, cell ranges, cells, charts, and so on. An object model is a description of the object hierarchy. Excel/VBA contains a clearly defined set of objects that are arranged according to relationships between them. Figure 4.1 shows a portion of the Excel object model. This is not complete but should give you an idea of the relationships between Excel objects. As we can see from Figure 4.1, the *Application* object is at the top level. Contained within the Application object are the Workbooks collection and all the Workbook instances within this; at the next lower level, we have the Worksheets collection along with the instances of each Worksheet in the collection. Next, we have the Range object, which does not have a plural collection.

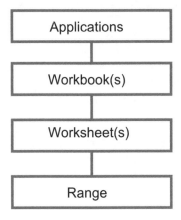

Figure 4.1 The hierarchy of some Excel objects

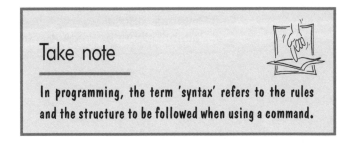

Take note

In programming, the term 'syntax' refers to the rules and the structure to be followed when using a command.

Referencing objects using With...End With

Sometimes, it may be necessary to refer to the same object properties or methods several times consecutively within a VBA macro. You can use a **With...End With** program structure that simplifies object reference.

The basic syntax of **With...End With** is:

```
With Object
    'Statements that use properties & methods of that object'
End With
```

To see how this works, suppose that we wanted to set the three properties with the interior of the object Range ("D34") as follows:

```
Range ("D34").ColorIndex = 3       'Sets the colour to red
Range ("D34").Pattern = xlSolid      'Makes the interior colour red solid
Range ("D34").PatternColorIndex = xlAutomatic
'This resets to automatic the colour following the selection
```

Instead of the longhand individual reference to each property or method of the range, we could rewrite the above using **With...End With** as follows:

```
Range ("D34").Select
    With Selection.Interior
        .ColorIndex = 3          'this colour is red
        .Pattern = xlSolid
        .PatternColorIndex = xlAutomatic
    End With
```

Note how the statements are indented between the **With Selection.Interior** and **End With** block.

Self-assessment exercise

Use the **With... End With** structure to rewrite the following lines:

```
Cell.ColourIndex =5
Cell.Pattern = xlSolid
Cell.PatternColorIndex = xlAutomatic
```

The Object Browser

The Object Browser provides the primary means to find objects and their associated properties and methods in Excel/VBA. It gives programmers a window to the object hierarchy in VBA and Excel, allowing them to inspect the objects available in VBA and Excel and their methods and properties. It can be accessed from the VBE either by clicking the Object Browser button on the Standard toolbar, or selecting **Object Browser** from the **View** menu.

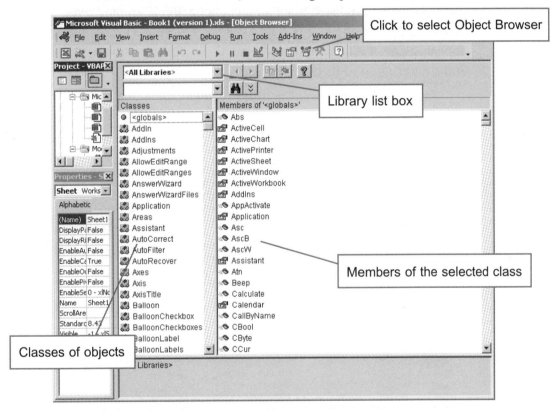

Figure 4.2 Selecting the Object Browser from the VBE

On entry to the Object Browser, you will see a screen similar to that in Figure 4.2. At the top left is a pull-down list of the Object model libraries, which includes the Excel and VBA library, as well as Office, VBA Project, and so on. The Excel library provides Help on all of the objects in the Excel object model, and their properties and methods. The VBA library provides Help on the VBA elements that are common to all applications that can use VBA, including Excel, Word, Access and PowerPoint. The default is *All Libraries*.

The left-hand pane lists all Classes of objects in the library, while the right-hand pane lists all the properties and methods associated with each selection. For example, Figure 4.4 shows a list of classes available with the Excel library. When a class is highlighted on the class list, then a complete list of properties and methods associated with it appears in the right-hand pane. Note that the Object Browser does not distinguish between properties and methods – they are listed together alphabetically. If an individual member of this list is highlighted (**ChartArea**, in Figure 4.3) then a description appears below this pane stating whether the selection is a property or method and a description of its use, such as:

```
Property ChartArea As ChartArea
   read-only
   Member of Excel.Chart
```

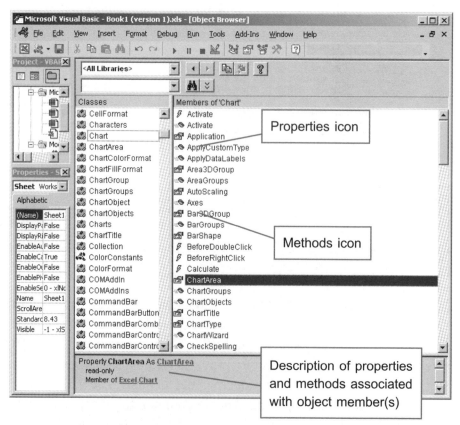

Figure 4.3 The Object Browser with an object and a property selected

Notice that properties are designated by the hand icon, whereas methods are indicated using a rectangular icon. The properties or methods of some objects may themselves be objects. For example, the **ChartArea** method of the **Chart** object in Figure 4.3 is itself an object and as such, the properties and methods of this object can be inspected (see Figure 4.4). One such method for this object is **Copy**.

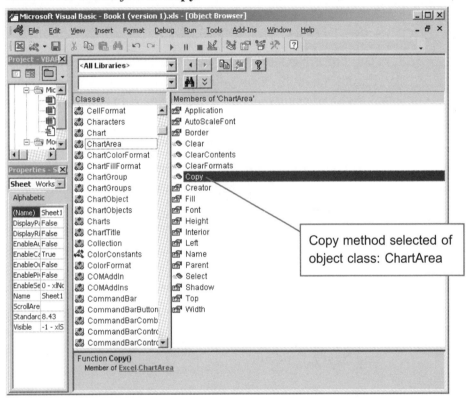

Figure 4.4 Working deeper into the Object Browser

How much knowledge of objects is necessary?

There are many objects available in Excel/VBA with all sorts of properties and methods. There are almost 200 objects in the Excel object model alone, and about 5000 properties and methods associated with these objects. Clearly, the reader could not be expected to become familiar with all of these. However, knowledge of the familiar objects like Application, Workbook,

Worksheet, Range and Chart are essential. Regarding the remaining objects in the libraries, it should be noted that experienced programmers are often faced with huge amounts of technical information about object libraries, and so on. They learn to develop ways of exploring the broad range of what is available, to have some idea of what may be useful in the future, and to know how to get the details when or if the need arises.

For Each ... Next Loop

The **For...Next** loop will be described in more detail in Chapter 7. It is introduced in this section in order for us to tackle important examples. The purpose of using the **For... Next** statements is to create a 'loop'. A loop is a construct that is repeated several times. This could be, for example, each worksheet in a workbook or each cell in a range, and so on.

The syntax of the **For Each ... Next** loop is:

```
For Each element In group
    statements
Next
```

For example:

```
For Each cell In Range ("Week_sales")
    Statements
Next
```

Notice how the statements between **For Each cell in Range ("week_sales")** and **Next** are indented.

Validating data

Consider the workbook SALESMAN. The following program is concerned with ensuring that data entered into the weekly sales range are strictly numeric values within a set range. This has been arbitrarily selected as between 0 and 100. A VBA program will need to scrutinise each cell in the weekly sales range and check to see that its value is numeric and within the range 0 to 100. Should a value be entered that is outside this valid range, then the program should respond with a message requesting that the user should input only acceptable data. The program is also required to colour any invalid cell red.

The structured English pseudocode follows:

Unprotect the Weekly Sales sheet
For each cell in the range Weekly Sales
    Check to see if the cell is Numeric
    If it is not, change its colour to red and display a message to the user
        to ensure the cell content is numeric
    Then check to see if the cell is within the range 0 to 100
    If it is not, change its colour to red and display a message to the user
        to ensure that the cell content is within the required limits.
    Otherwise leave alone and go on to the next cell in the range

The purpose of the following VBA macro is to validate the data in the range *week_sales* so that if any cell in this range is either not numeric or if it is outside the range 0–100, then a message will alert the user. Furthermore, the offending cell will be solidly coloured red.

Listing 4.2 Validating Data in the week_sales Range

```
' Validate Week_sales data input
' checks that data input in the week sales is a number in the range 0-100
Sub validateWeekSales()
    Dim Cell As Object
    Worksheets("Weeklysales").select
    For Each Cell In Range("Week_sales")
        If Not IsNumeric(Cell) Then
            MsgBox "Please enter a number in cell " &Cell.Address
            With Cell.Interior
                .ColorIndex = 3
                .Pattern = xlSolid
                .PatternColorIndex = xlAutomatic
            End With
        ElseIf (Cell < 0) Or (Cell > 100) Then
            MsgBox "Please enter number between 0 & 100 in cell "
                & Cell.Address
            With Cell.Interior
                .ColorIndex = 3
                .Pattern = xlSolid
                .PatternColorIndex = xlAutomatic
            End With
        End If
    Next
End Sub
```

Notes on Listing 4.2

The purpose of this program is to validate the *week_sales* range data input to ensure that each item in the range is both numeric and between the range 0–100. The VBA macro has been called *validateWeekSales*.

```
Dim cell as Object
```

declares that cell is an Object. The purpose of this line will become more meaningful when we look at variables in Chapter 5.

```
Worksheets("Weeklysales").select
```

will ensure that the ActiveSheet is the Weeklysales worksheet.

```
For Each Cell in Range("week_sales")
```

takes each cell in the range of cells called *week_sales* in order to do something to it. You will see that there is a **Next** line later in the program. Any use of a **For** statement must terminate with a **Next** statement. This is because the **For** statement tells the macro to repeat some lines a number of times (in this case the number of cells in the range *week_sales*), this means the program needs to know at what point the next cell in the range is to be selected. Chapter 7 will look in more detail at statements using **For... Next**.

```
If Not IsNumeric(Cell)
```

will test to see if the cell is numeric. This uses an **If...Then** structure (see in more detail in Chapter 6). The purpose of this statement is to check to see if each cell in the range is not numeric; if it is not then the following statements will be executed:

```
MsgBox "Please enter a number in cell " &Cell.Address
With  Cell.Interior
   .ColorIndex = 3
   .Pattern = xlSolid
   .PatternColorIndex = xlAutomatic
End  With
```

In the line following this the ranges is tested:

```
ElseIf (Cell < 0) Or (Cell > 100) Then
```

and if the number is invalid, the cell's colour and pattern are set to show the error.

The **With** construct was described earlier in this chapter.

The next line **Next** was described a little earlier.

Finally, the program terminates with an End Sub line.

Figure 4.5 gives a screenshot during the macro run.

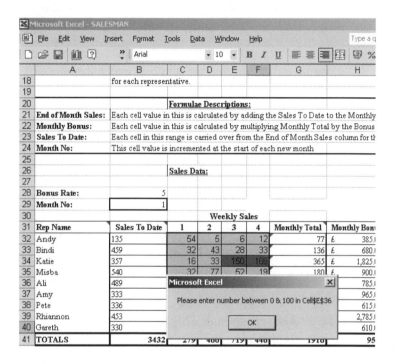

Figure 4.5 Screenshot of Listing 4.2 during program run

Referencing named ranges

There are a number of ways to reference a range in VBA. Some of these are:

- Using a named range – follow the Range object with the named range in double quotation marks. For example, **Range("week_sales")**

- Use a cell address range – the same as above, but use a cell address reference range. For example, **Range("D1:D5")**

- Use a Range object variable (see Chapter 5). To create a Range object variable called *myRange*, you can use statements of the following form:

    ```
    Dim RandomRange As Range
    Set RandomRange = Range("b1:b10")
    ```

- Use the *Cells* property of the Range object. This property can be used with either one or two arguments. For example, you could write: **Range ("week_sales").Cells (5)**. If we look at Figure 4.5, the value returned will be 32, because this is the value of the contents of the cell in the fifth position of this range. Note that rectangular ranges are scanned from row to row. You can also use the Cells property with two arguments. For example, if we had **Range ("week_sales").Cells (2, 3)** then the value returned from this cell would be 66, because this is the value of the second row, third column cell in the range *week_sales*.

- Use the **Offset** method. This method works with two arguments and has the form **Offset(x,y)** where *x* is the rowOffset – the number of rows to go down (up if x is <0), and y is the columnOffset – the number of columns across to the right (to the left if y<0).

    For example, in Figure 4.5, *Range("rep_name").Offset(0,1)* would begin in the range *rep_name* and the rowOffset is 0, but the columnOffset is 1. This means it would actually refer to the next column to the right (because it is +1), and therefore the *sales_to_date* range.

Some examples using the Range object

The following macro is used to create a named range variable called *RandomRange* in Excel. A **For… Next** loop is then used to generate a set of random numbers in each cell in *RandomRange*. After completion of the **For…Next** loop, the cell values are then sorted using the **Sort** method. A screenshot of the output is shown in Figure 4.6.

Listing 4.3

```
Sub cellProperty ()
    Dim RandomRange As Range
    Set RandomRange = Range("b1:b10")
    For Each cell In RandomRange
        cell.Value = Int(Rnd() * 20 + 1)
    Next
    RandomRange.Sort key1:=RandomRange
End Sub
```

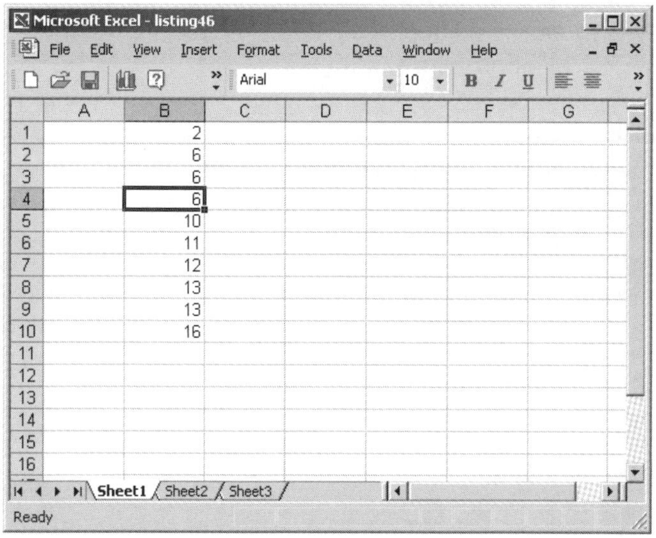

Figure 4.6 Screenshot of the output

This next example will format the worksheet named *Summary* from the SALESMAN workbook. The screenshot displayed in Figure 4.7 is taken before the macro in Listing 4.4 is run. You will see from the screenshot that Column B displays each rep name and columns C and D contain numbers which are supposed to represent the highest and lowest sales respectively for the rep during the last six month period. The macro will insert two new rows above the first rep name. It should insert appropriate headings in the rows immediately above the columns shown. These should be "Name", "Highest Sales" and "Lowest Sales" respectively. There should also be data in column E that contains a formula that calculates the difference between the highest and lowest sales. The VBA code is shown in Listing 4.4.

Listing 4.4

```
Sub formatSummarySheet()
   Worksheets ("Summary").Select
   Range ("A1").Select
   With Selection
   .EntireRow.Insert
   .EntireRow.Insert
   End With
   Range ("B2").Value = "Rep Name"
   Range ("C2").Value = "Highest Sales"
   Range ("D2").Value = "Lowest Sales"
   Range ("E2").Value = "Difference"
   Range ("E3:E11").Formula = "=C3-D3"
End Sub
```

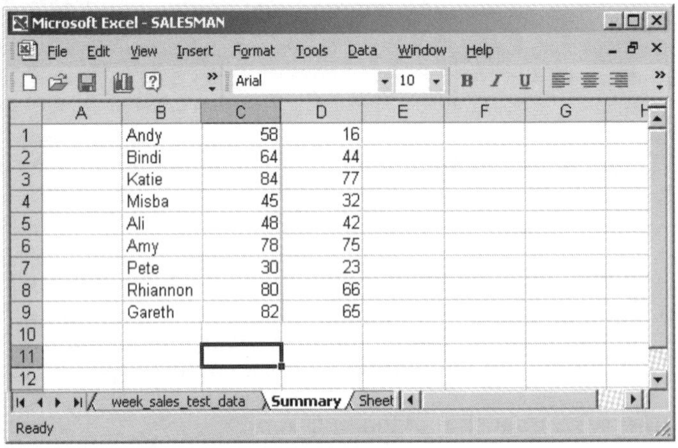

Figure 4.7 Summary Worksheet Data

The VBA procedure is named *formatSummarySheet* and the first statement selects the required *Summary* worksheet. The next statement selects the range A1 ready for the insertion of the new rows using the *EntireRow.Insert* object reference. **Range ("B2").Value = "Rep Name"** sets the value in cell B2 to "Rep Name", as do the three other statements set the other headings. The statement **Range ("E3:E11").Formula = "=C3-D3"** assigns a relative formula to each cell in the range E3:E11, to the difference between the highest and lowest sales figure for each rep name. When the macro is run, the worksheet *Summary* is shown in Figure 4.8.

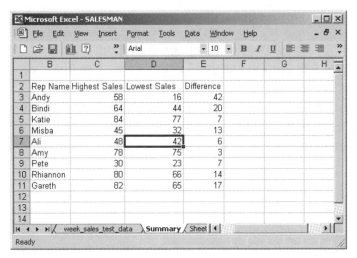

Figure 4.8 Screenshot of Listing 4.4 output

More on methods

The **Offset** method of the **Range** object has been mentioned in the previous section. It is tempting to think of Offset as a property. It isn't for if it were, it would have to store all its neighbours inside itself – that would be a waste of memory, but it can 'go and look for its neighbours' if it is told to. When you use Offset you are telling it to 'go and look for your neighbour(s)'. Hence, Offset is a method, not a property.

```
myCell.Offset (0, -8)
```

Objects are more complex than the base types or the user-defined types. They have both properties and methods (attributes and behaviour).

The properties are a bit like base type variables contained within the object. For example, you've been setting the **.ColorIndex** of a cell's **.Interior** to some number like 5 or 28. So: **interior** is an object with a property called **ColorIndex** which is an integer.

```
myCell.Interior.ColorIndex = 3
```

Some useful Application object methods

The Application object includes these useful methods and properties.

- *DisplayAlerts* allows you to turn off a warning message using a statement of the form Application.DisplayAlerts = False. Use this if you want to prevent a warning message from appearing whenever you delete a worksheet. You can turn it back on with the line Application.DisplayAlerts = True. Use with care for though warning messages can irritate us, we certainly miss them if we inadvertently delete work which has taken much effort on our part.

- *Cursor* is a property. Sometimes, when a lengthy macro is running, the cursor will change to an hourglass, then momentarily back to normal, only to resume a *wait* status again. Users sometimes find this irritating. The statement: *Application. Cursor = xlWait* turns the cursor to an hourglass. *Application. Cursor = xlNormal* restores the cursor to normal.

- The *ScreenUpdating* property relates to the display. The statement: *Application.ScreenUpdating = False* will freeze the screen while a macro runs and thus prevent any flickering. The screen will remain frozen until you assign the property value back to *True*, or when the macro finishes executing.

- *InputBox* is a method that uses the Application object to prompt for a range. The following statement illustrates its use:

```
myRange = Application.InputBox (prompt: = "Enter the range required",
    Type: = 8)
```

The InputBox method may look similar to the InputBox function which we looked at in Chapter 3, however, it is very different in practice. The InputBox method of the Application object here has a more flexible format than the InputBox function, in that we can specify the type of data that has to be input via the dialog box. For example, in the statement above we have specified Type: = 8, meaning that the data input is expected to be a cell range. If the user attempts to input anything other than a cell range, it will not be accepted and will invoke an error message. This is very useful if you want to restrict the type of data that can be used with a program input. More examples that use the InputBox Application object method will be given in Chapter 6. Note that the user can type in the cell range in the usual format, or can select the range using the mouse.

Exercises

1   Open a new workbook. Using the default Sheet1, enter the values into the cell range A1 to A5 the numbers 3, 11, 9, 12, and 5 respectively. Now enter the following macro using the VBE:

```
Sub GreaterThanTen()
    Dim thisCell as Object
    For each cell in Range ("A1:A5")
        If thisCell >10 Then
            MsgBox "Another One Found"
            thisCell.Font.Bold =True
        End If
    Next
End Sub
```

Explain what you think this program may be doing. Run the macro and check, using the data given to see that it works properly.

2   Using the macro that you have written in Exercise 1, describe each line of code that contains an object reference. Identify properties and methods in the references.

3   Use the Object Browser to look up the Range object and find out about the property or method called Cells. State whether it is a property or a method.

4   Given the same worksheet data as in Exercise 1, state the following property value:

```
Range ("A1:A5").Cells (3)
```

5   Explain what the following section of code is doing:

```
Charts (1).Activate
With ActiveChart
    .Type = xlLine
    .HasTitle = True
    .ChartTitle.Text = "February Week Sales"
End With
```

6   Open the SALESMAN workbook and make the *weeklysales* sheet active. Now create and run a macro to reset the color of all the cells in the week_sales range to the colour light grey. (**Hint**: Use the **With...End With** construct that was used in Listing 4.2, and set the ColorIndex = 15). Check to see that it has run correctly.

7   Open the SALESMAN workbook and make the *weeklysales* sheet active. Now design pseudocode, and from it, create a new macro that will check each cell in the *end_month_sales* range and if their sales have exceeded 200, then set a border of medium thickness around the cell.

Create another macro using the SALESMAN workbook that will check the same as above, but this time instead of setting a medium thickness border around the *end_month_sales* cells that are greater than 200; it will instead set the border around the corresponding salesperson. (**Hint**: Use the same macro code as above, but this time use the Offset method to reference the corresponding salesperson position in the worksheet).

5 Variables

What are variables? 92

Variable declarations 96

Explicit and implicit declarations . . 97

Assigning values to variables 99

VBA program using variables . . . 101

Using constants in VBA 104

User defined data types 105

Using arrays in VBA 107

Exercises 111

What are variables?

Cells in Excel worksheets enable us to store visible data items of all kinds. However, sometimes when an Excel application is running we might need to store data in temporary memory locations other than cells. For example, suppose we wanted to write a macro that searches through the list of representatives for a particular name? To do this, we would need to input this name into a temporary location, so that the macro could check each item in the name range. Such locations are called *variables*. Variables are one of the most ubiquitous concepts of any programming language. They are used to represent named areas in the memory of a computer where data can be stored.

Declaring and assigning variables

Each variable has a name – something that is decided by the programmer. The programmer also decide what type of data it will hold. For example, if a variable is to store a person's age, a whole number – or *integer* – might be appropriate, as people normally give their age as an integer, such as 45 or 38.

Each variable is of a particular type. The type is designated by the programmer in a process known as *declaration*. A variable can be given a value – this is called *assignment* – and that value can be retrieved later. It may be helpful to picture a variable as a tiny box inside the computer as shown here.

NAME	age
DATA TYPE	Integer
VALUE	48

The diagram shows that the variable named *age* has been declared as an Integer data type, and the variable currently contains the value 48.

One can also think of a variable as a spreadsheet cell that is not visible to the user. After all, a cell can contain a data item that can be varied. However, using variables, rather than cells, allows VBA programs to run faster, for VBA can manipulate variables more efficiently. Moreover, variables can be used to hold (or save) temporary data when a macro is executing.

Variables are normally declared before the executable statements of a VBA program begin. We will look at the way in which variables can be assigned values a little later.

Variable types in VBA

When a name has been assigned to a variable, the programmer should decide what data type is to be assigned to it, as this defines what sort of data the variable may hold. For example, if we wanted to declare a variable that is going to hold a person's age it would best be a whole number –an integer. The variable would then be declared as type *Integer* and could be said to be an integer variable. A variable that holds textual data, such as a person's address would be declared as a *String* data type. A variable holding currency data, such as the cost of an item in a supermarket would be *Currency*. There are many other data types available in VBA, and Table 5.1 lists them all.

Table 5.1 Data types in Visual Basic for Applications for Excel

Data type	Description of range	Size in bytes
Boolean	Logical values: True or False	2 (16 bits)
Integer	-32768 to 32767	2 (16 bits)
Long	-2,147,483,648 to 2,147,483,647	4 (32 bits)
Single	Single precision floating point i.e. Negative numbers from: -3.402823 X 1038 to -1.401298 X 10-45 Positive numbers from: 1.401298. X 10-45 to 3.402823 X 1038	4 (32 bits)
Double	Double precision floating point	8 (64 bits)
Currency	Accurate fixed point calculation	8 (64 bits)
Date	Stores date and time information. Dates range from Jan 1, 100 : Dec 31, 9999. Times range from 00:00:00 to 23:59:59.	8 (64 bits)
Object	Used to access any object recognised by VBA	4 (32 bits)
String	Stores text. "abc ABC 123 !@£"	1 per char
Variant	Can store any other data type. Range depends on the data stored. If text, the range is of type String. If numeric, the range is of type Double.	16 + 1 per char
Array	Multidimensional data type. Each array element is of the same base type. i.e. integer, string, long etc.	Variable
User-defined	Data structures	Variable

An integer variable is assigned two bytes of memory. This gives a range of possible values of between –32768 and +32767 but this is not enough for some integer values. VBA therefore includes another integer data type called *Long* that assigns four bytes of memory. The choice between Integer and Long, will clearly depend on what range of values are likely to be represented by the variable. If the range of possible values is –32768 to 32767 then a data type Integer could be assigned to that variable. However, if a variable is to be used which is likely to store an integer value outside this range, then the data type would have to be Long. Similarly, when deciding on a choice between Single, Double, and Currency, the programmer should consider the likely data range taking extreme possibilities into consideration.

If in doubt about the choice of data type to assign to a variable, choose the maximum size data type.

A variable declared as a *String* data type may contain any text characters: alphabetic, numeric digits, punctuation characters, or other ASCII character symbols. A string size can be *fixed* or *variable* (see the examples that follow). Variable length, as the name suggests, permits a string to be of any length. The fixed length is assigned by the programmer – for example a string assigned to a person's name might be fixed length 20 characters. When a name is assigned to a fixed length string is shorter than the fixed length, then the remainder of the string is padded with spaces to reach the correct length. The default value for an unassigned string variable is "". While the default value for an assigned string variable is the number of spaces corresponding to the fixed size for a fixed length string.

Notice that VBA also includes a generic *Object* data type. It is possible to declare any Excel object using this type, but it is more efficient programming to restrict the object to a specific class declaration where possible. For example, if the programmer knows that a declared variable is going to be a Range object, then it is better to declare that variable as a Range data type rather than a generic Object data type. The reason is that Excel cannot tell what specific type of object it is using until the program is running. This is known as *late binding* and some execution time is wasted in making this determination. If the programmer has not declared the data type, then VBA will assign default declaration to *Variant*. The default value is *Empty*.

Rules for naming variables

A variable can be given any name as long as it satisfies the following rules:

- Variable names must begin with a letter of the alphabet
- After the first letter, the name for the variable may consist of any combination of digits, alphabetic letters or underscore characters – but no other characters are permitted.
- A variable name cannot exceed 256 characters in length.
- A variable name cannot be the same as an object method, property, VB function, procedure, argument name or a VBA reserved word.

Data type prefixes

Many programmers create variable names by using data type prefix such as cur (for currency) and sng (for single-precision). It is good practice to use data type prefixes in your variable names, although in the examples throughout this book I have not done so because most of the macros that are written are relatively short. Adopting this approach means you must type a little extra, but your program code will become more transparent.

Tip

Use meaningful variable names when writing VBA programs. By doing this, program code will be easier to understand and easier to maintain. Many programmers use the underscore character (_) to separate distinct words or capital letters, e.g. First_Name, Age_Of_Candidate, number_of_books, and so on.

Variable declarations

Variables are declared using the following syntax:

Dim　　NameOfVariable　　As　　DataType

The following examples illustrate the way that variables are declared in VBA programs. Declarations are usually written in a VBA program, before program execution statements begin. Notice in the following examples how comments have been attached to the right of each declaration line to improve readability.

```
Dim theTotal As Long              'declared as a long integer variable
Dim aName As String               'variable length string declaration
Dim fName As String * 20          'fixed length size 20 characters
Dim lastDayOfTerm As Date         'Date variable declaration
Dim dataSheet As Worksheet        'Worksheet object declaration
Dim studentPresent As Boolean     'Boolean variable, (TRUE or FALSE)

Dim TopCell As Range              'Range object declaration
Dim theCell As Object             'generic Object declaration
Dim salesChart As Chart           'specific object Chart declaration
```

Self-assessment exercise

What data type would you assign to a variable that is going to store?

a) The weight of a bunch of carrots in kilograms?

b) The number of people present at a rugby match?

c) The distance between galaxies in miles?

Tip

It is good practice to declare all variables before the executable statements in a VBA program begin. By declaring all variable names together at the beginning of a procedure it becomes easier to find a variable name if required. Later in this chapter we will see that it is possible to force the programmer to declare variables.

Explicit and implicit declarations

The VBA default data type is the Variant data type. As Table 5.1 shows, a variable of the variant data type consumes 16 bytes plus 1 for each character, and is used to store a data item when the data type is not known. Using a Variant data type can be costly in memory and program execution time. Lomax (see Further reading, page 218) estimates that expressions using only Variant data execute about 30% slower than the same expressions using the correct intrinsic data types. In VBA, the programmer is **not** required to declare a variable type explicitly, but it is advisable to do so for these reasons:

◆ It gives clarity to program design; the programmer will better understand the purpose of each variable when they are explicitly declared.

◆ It prevents inadvertent creation of new variables by misspelling the name of an existing one; this will make debugging easier since any spelling errors will be identified before program compilation.

◆ It makes code easier to understand by grouping all variable names at the beginning of a program.

◆ Code is executed faster if the correct data type is assigned to each variable. This is because they will consume less memory, and therefore be retrieved more quickly.

◆ Less memory is required if the correct data type is assigned to each variable.

Option explicit

A programmer can force all variable declarations in a program by inserting an *Option Explicit* command before the procedure definition begins. By inserting this optional command, the VBA program will expect every variable that is used in the program to be declared before it can be used. This is good VBA program practice. An example of Option Explicit follows:

```
Option Explicit
'Notice how the option explicit command precedes the procedure
definition all variables must be declared

Sub thisProg ()
Dim salesChart As Chart
'Specific object Chart declaration must be declared
Dim theTotal As Long
' this variable must be declared since Option explicit has been used
```

```
Dim myDaughtersName As String
' this variable must also be declared
```

Setting explicit declarations for variables

You can set VBA for Excel to so that you are forced to declare all variables explicitly without having to write an Option Explicit line in every program. This can be done either globally (for all modules) or on a module by module basis. To do this, choose **Tools > Options** from the VBE. You will see the **Options** dialog box. Click the **Editor** tab, and tick the **Require Variable Declaration** box (see Figure 5.1). Notice, that it is unchecked by default. Now, if you do this, you will find an Option Explicit appear for each new module that you create.

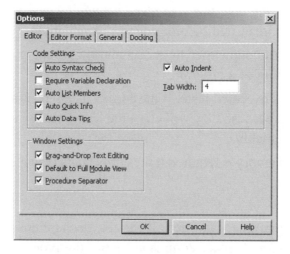

Figure 5.1 Setting the explicit variable declaration requirement

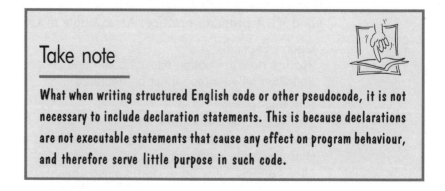

Take note

What when writing structured English code or other pseudocode, it is not necessary to include declaration statements. This is because declarations are not executable statements that cause any effect on program behaviour, and therefore serve little purpose in such code.

Assigning values to variables

A variable declaration tells VBA what type of data a variable can hold, but the purpose of creating variables is to store values in them (see Table 5.2). This section shows how values can be assigned to a variable. The following examples illustrate how variables of different types can be assigned values. Note that literal strings are enclosed in "double quotes". Dates are enclosed in #hashes#. Values of a Boolean variable are assigned as *True* or *False*.

```
NameOfVariable = value
NoOfNectarPoints  =  5000              'Integer assignment
MyDaughtersName  =  "Rhiannon"         'String assignment
lastDayOfTerm  =  #3 Apr 2003#
'To enter literal date values, place # before and after the date
studentPresent  =  TRUE                ' Boolean assignment
Set TopCell  =  Range("A1")
'This assignment is slightly different - note the use of Set
'this associates a worksheet range with TopCell
```

Take care when using assignment statements. To understand why, consider the statements $x = y$ and $y = x$. While being algebraically the same, they are not the same assignments and will produce different results. For example, if the content of variable x is 10 and the content of y is 25, then $\mathbf{x} = \mathbf{y}$ will result in both variables taking the value 25, since $\mathbf{x} = \mathbf{y}$ means x is assigned the content of y (25). On the other hand, $\mathbf{y} = \mathbf{x}$ will result in both variables taking the value 10, since y is assigned the content of x which is 10.

Table 5.2 Summary of how variables are declared and assigned in VBA.

Name	Type	Value	Type declaration in VBA	How assigned in VBA
LastDayOfTerm	Date	3 Apr 2003	Dim LastDayOfTerm As Date	LastDayOfTerm = #3/4/2003#
MyDaughtersName	String	Rhiannon	Dim MyDaughtersName as String	MyDaughtersName = "Rhiannon"
NoOfNectarPoints	Integer	5000	Dim NoOfNectarPoints As Integer	NoOfNectarPoints = 5000
TopCell	Range	Cell A1	Dim TopCell As Range	Set TopCell = Range("A1")

The following example declares a date variable called *LastDayOfTerm* and assigns it the value 3/4/2003 (3rd April 2003). The date is then displayed in a MsgBox (see Figure 5.2).

```
Sub dateShow ()
    Dim LastDayOfTerm As Date
    LastDayOfTerm = #3/4/2003#
    MsgBox LastDayOfTerm
```

Figure5.2 The Date MsgBox Output in American Format

The Set keyword

As the last example in Table 5.2 shows, the difference between assigning a value to an object variable and a non-object variable is that the object assignment must begin with the keyword **Set.** The remainder of the syntax is identical to that when declaring a non-object variable. For example, the following two lines of VBA code declare a variable called *this_month_sales* as a Range object, and define it with the keyword Set.

```
Dim this_month_sales As Range
Set this_month_sales = Range ("month_sales")
```

The above two lines will assign the range variable *this_month_sales* to the range variable *month_sales*.

Self-assessment exercise

Write two lines of code that will assign the chart variable *my_new_chart* to the chart variable *my_chart*.

Take note

When a variable appears on both sides of an assignment's equal sign, the variable is being updated in some way. For example, the statement: Number = Number +1 will result in the variable *Number* being assigned the existing value of that variable plus 1.

VBA program using variables

VBA Listing 5.1 includes line numbers for ease of explanation. Do not include these in any VBA for Excel code.

Listing 5.1 VBA program using variables

```
1    Option Explicit      'forces the programmer to declare all variables
2    Sub sumValues()
3        Dim first_number As Integer    'declare 3 variables as integers
4        Dim second_number As Integer
5        Dim sum As Integer
6        Dim Result As Range
7        first_number = InputBox(prompt:="enter first number")
8        second_number = InputBox(prompt:="enter second number")
9        sum = first_number + second_number
10       Worksheets(1).Select
11       Columns("B:B").ColumnWidth = 18
12       Range("B1").Font.Bold = True
13       Range("B1").Value = "Number Adding Program"
14       Range("B3:B5").Clear
15       Range("B3").Value = "First Number ="
16       Range("B4").Value = "Second Number ="
17       Range("B5").Value = "Sum ="
18       Range("C3:C5").Clear
19       Range ("C3").Value = first_number
20       Range ("C4").Value = second_number
21       Set Result = Range ("C5")
22       Result.Value = sum
23       Result.Font.Bold = True
24       Result.Borders (xlBottom).Weight = xlMedium
25       Result.Borders (lop).Weight = xlMedium
26   End Sub
```

Listing 5.1 is a VBA program that enables a user to input two numbers, and output the result along with the numbers on a blank spreadsheet (see Figure 5.3). The program assigns two integer variables called *first_number* and *second_number* using input boxes. The sum of these variables after input is then assigned to another integer variable called *sum*. Each of these variables is then assigned to worksheet cells in the range C3 to C5, along with appropriate labels in the previous column cell range (i.e. B3 to B5) and a heading which begins in cell B1.

Lines 3 to 5 declares the integer variables *first_number*, *second_number* and *sum*.

Line 6 declares the range object variable *result* which will store the output (i.e. transfer the *sum*) to a cell range.

Lines 7 and 8 use input boxes to input values into the variables *first_number* and *second_number*.

Line 9 assigns *first_number* + *second_number* to the variable *sum*.

Line 10 selects a new blank worksheet to present the results.

Line 11 adjusts the column width to make it big enough for the new text.

Line 12 makes the heading in cell B1 bold.

Line 13 inserts the text heading.

Line 14 clears the cell range B3 to B5 ready for the text labels which are inserted with lines 15 to 17.

Line 18 clears the cell range C3 to C5.

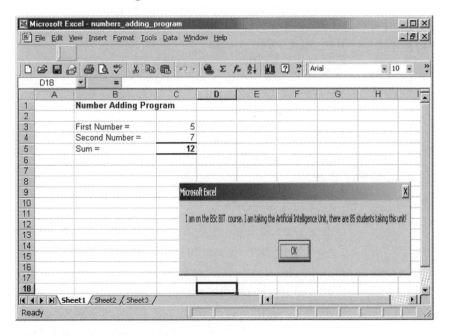

Figure 5.3 Addition program output in Excel

Line 19 puts the value of *first_number* into cell C3 and line 20 puts the value of *second_number* into cell C4.

Line 21 then Line 22 sets C5 with the variable called *result*.

Line 23 puts the value of sum into *result* – i.e. into C5.

Lines 24 and 25 set the top and bottom border of the cell C5 to a medium weight by assigning the xlMedium constant to the Weight property of the object Borders (which is a property of a Range object).

You should study the VBA program carefully to ensure that you clearly understand the output in Figure 5.3.

Self assessment exercise

Identify all other object properties that exist in the Listing 5.1.

Using constants in VBA

Sometimes it is convenient to name a data item that is used in a macro as a fixed or *constant* value. For example, the speed of light has a constant numerical value of 186,000 miles per second. If we were writing a macro that referenced this constant, we could name it in the same way that we name variables. However, it would clearly differ from a variable in that its value remains constant. You can do this by using the syntax shown below. Examples of the way in which constants are declared are also shown below:

```
Const ConstName As Integer = value
    Const Speed_Of_Light As Integer = 186000
    Const Min_Age_For_Alcohol As Integer = 18
    Const Pie As Single = 3.142
    Const Pound_Euro_Exchange_Rate As Single = 1.4
```

There are good reasons for using named constants rather than direct numerical values in VBA programs:

♦ Any changes made to a constant only have to be made once in the program. For example, if a program has the constant *Pound_Euro_Exchange_Rate* and the actual rate rises to 1.5, then you only need change the 1.4 to 1.5.

♦ The greater readability of the code makes program maintenance easier.

Take note

A constant, like a variable, is a named item, but unlike a variable, it retains the same value throughout the execution of a program.

User-defined data types

A number of VBA ' built-in' data types such as Integer, Double and String have been introduced in this chapter. These are called *base types*. Sometimes these are not adequate. For example, suppose you wanted a data type to represent the actual days of the week, as names in an ordered list. Or what if you wanted a data type representing a record in a customer database? There are no base types in VBA that could be used directly to represent these data structures, but it is possible for the programmer to create new data types describing them. These are known as *user-defined* data types. Once created, we can manipulate these user-defined types directly by creating variables, or constants, of that data type throughout the program for which it is defined.

Creating a user-defined data type

A new data type can be defined using the *Type* statement. In example below a user-defined type is required to represent an employee record. Notice how multiple variables have been combined into a single variable – each part is known as a 'field' (like a property of an object). When the definition is complete, an *End Type* statement is required. Variables of the new data type may then be used in exactly the same way as a normal base type variable, that is, using the Dim statement. The syntax creating a user-defined data type is:

```
Type   Name
       FieldName1 As ...
       FieldName2 As...
       Etc...
End Type
```

An example of creating a user-defined data type and variable of that type:

```
'this example defines a new data type called Employee Record

Type  EmployeeRecord
   FirstName As String * 10
    'First field, called FirstName is fixed length 10 characters
   LastName As String * 20    'LastName is fixed length 20 characters
   TelNumber  As String * 12  'TelNumber, fixed length 12 characters
   Salary  As Currency        'Fourth item in record is called Salary
   StartDate As Date          'Last item is called StartDate
End Type

'The next part shows how to use the new data type – i.e. declaring
variables of that type to use in the macro
```

```
Dim anEmployee As EmployeeRecord     'declaration of variable
anEmployee.FirstName = "John"
'assignment - i.e. put John into the FirstName field
```

The above fragment illustrates how a data type called *EmployeeRecord* is defined and how a new variable (*anEmployee*) of this data type can be created. A component of this variable has been assigned for use in the program, e.g. *anEmployee.FirstName = "John"*.

Listing 5.2 gives an example of a VBA macro using a user defined type.

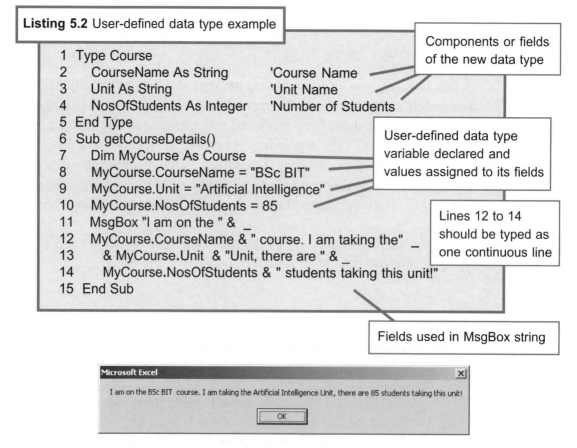

Figure 5. 4 Screenshot of user-defined type example

106

Using arrays in VBA

An array is a set of data items that are stored in contiguous memory locations all of which have the same name and the same data type. A particular data item is *referenced* by specifying the array and the element position number (the *index*). Names that are given to arrays are subject to the same rules as any other variable. The elements of the array can be of any data type. For example, Figure 5.5 shows a *five-element currency* array called *expenses*. Any one of the elements in this array may be referenced by giving the array name followed by the index in parentheses, (). The index numbering starts at 0, though we tend to think of positions as starting at 1. Thus, the element at position 1 is written as *expenses(0)*. The element at position 2 is written as *expenses(1)*, the element at position 3, *expenses(2)*, and so on. In general the element at position n is written as *expenses(n-1)*.

expenses (0)	expenses (1)	expenses (2)	expenses (3)	expenses (4)
$20.50	$35.50	$38.25	$65.40	$54.35

Figure 5.5 A five-element array called *expenses*

Declaring an array

An array is declared in a similar way to any other variable. The only difference is that the size (or **Dim**ension) of the array must be written in parentheses after the variable name.

```
Dim  NameOfArray (ArrayLength)  As    DataType
```

The following example declares two arrays. In the first, for an array called *expenses*, each of the five elements is a Currency variable. In the second, for an array called *employee*, each of the 20 elements is a String variable.

```
Dim expenses (5)  As  Currency
'expenses  is declared as a five-element currency array variable

Dim  employee(20)  As  String
'employee is declared as a twenty-element long String  variable
```

An array can be *populated* with a series of values by using the Array function. For example, the expenses array is populated as follows:

```
Expenses = Array (20.50, 35.50, 38.25, 65.40, 54.35)
```

An array can also be populated using a **For...Next** loop (see next example).

Dynamic arrays

Our declarations so far have been of the form:

```
Dim expenses (5) As Currency
```

This statement shows that the array called expenses contains 5 fixed elements, and that the lower and upper bounds of the array index are 0 to 4: meaning that the starting index is 0 and the highest index is 4. However, there are some situations that arise in which the size of an array would be unknown to the programmer in advance of writing the program. For example, if an array was going to itself contain a variable number of data items. A dynamic array can be declared to deal with this situation. It is declared just like any other array, except that the parentheses are empty. Hence, a dynamic currency array called *expenses*, would be declared as:

```
Dim expenses () As Currency
```

A dynamic array can be resized using the *ReDim* statement, as in:

```
ReDim expenses (10)
```

Arrays are primarily used to deal with lists. The following example is typical of the use of arrays. The SALESMAN workbook uses a macro to add the five working weekdays to get a total for the weekly mileage. The figure is then entered into the ActiveCell (this must be in the range *WeekSales* in order that it can be used). The program outputs, using a **MsgBox**, the daily mileages that were entered and a chance to change any of the values in case there was an error during entry. The user will be prompted with a **MsgBox** that will contain **Yes** and **No** options. Should the user select **No**, the program will ask them to re-enter the data again until they respond with **Yes** in the **MsgBox**. After this the program will then respond with another **MsgBox** stating the total for the daily sales. The program will also enter this value in the ActiveCell of the blank worksheet *Sheet2*. Although this could be done without the use of arrays, they make the job easier. Listing 5.3 shows how this program would work.

This example uses an array to store the daily sales for an employee. This is done by reading the data into an array using the **InputBox** function. These items are then added to get a week sales total. The result is placed in the ActiveCell in the *Sheet2* (a temporary location). In the declaration section, the array called *thisDaySales(5)* has been declared as an Integer array. After

Listing 5.3 Using an array to total daily sales

```
Sub totalDailySales()
'Adds together five items of data to get a week sales total for the employee.
'For each working day
    Dim answerStr As String
    Dim totalSales As Integer
    Dim answerNo As Integer
    Dim thisDaySales (5) As Integer
    Dim dayCount As Integer
    answerStr = ""
    TotalSales = 0
    Worksheets ("Sheet2").Select
    Do
      For dayCount = 1 To 5
        thisDaySales (dayCount) = InputBox(prompt:= "enter sales for day: "
            & dayCount)
        totalSales = totalSales + thisDaySales(dayCount)
      Next
      For dayCount = 1 To 5
         AnswerStr = Str (thisDaySales (dayCount)) + answerStr
      Next
      AnswerStr = "Do you want to change these values?" +answerStr
      answerNo = MsgBox (answerStr, 4, "Check daily Mileages")
    Loop Until answerNo = 7
    ActiveCell.Value = totalSales   'set value of the active cell to total sales
    ActiveCell.Offset (0, -1).ColumnWidth = 14
    'extend the column width in the left cell, so complete label will be visible
    ActiveCell.Offset (0, -1).Value = "Total Sales ="
    'insert "Total Sales" in this cell
End Sub
```

declaring all the variables, the line **Worksheets ("Sheet3").Select** will select the *Sheet2* for storing the final result.

The purpose of the **Do…Until** loop is to allow the user the chance to check the correctness of the data entered posting the total to the ActiveCell on the *weeklysales* worksheet. (Loops will be studied in more detail in Chapter 7.) Notice how two **For…Next** loops are used in sequence in this program. The first is used to read the daily sales data into the array called *thisDaySales*. The second is used to create a string variable called *answerStr*. The purpose of the *answerStr* variable is to contain the sequence of data input for the five daily sales; data stored as a string is easier to output with a **MsgBox** statement. The variable *answerNo* that is used for the **MsgBox** response will contain the values **Yes** or **No**. The **Loop Until answerNo = 7** line will test to see if the value **No** has been chosen. When it has, the loop will terminate and the contents of the *totalSales* variable will be written to the active cell of the *week_sales* range of the worksheet. The program will then terminate.

There are three screenshots showing action points during the program run. Figure 5.6 shows a **InputBox** request for day 2. Figure 5.7 shows the **MsgBox** that displays the data for the five days. Notice that this box lets the user correct any mistakes by retyping the data set. Figure 5.8 displays the *Sheet2* display after the user has accepted the data in the **MsgBox**.

Figure 5.6 Entering daily data for the VBA program Listing 5.5

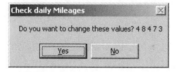

Figure 5.7 MsgBox output showing the daily values from program Listing 5.5

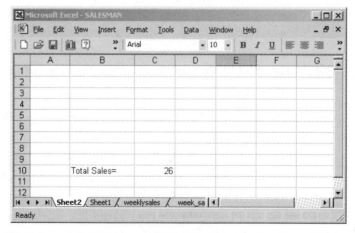

Figure 5.8 Value of TotalSales and label in left hand column in Sheet2

Exercises

1   Examine the following entities and consider what data types you would use to represent them as variables in a VBA program:

*   the cost of a colour television
*   the number of pages in a book
*   the temperature in a freezer cabinet
*   someone's presence or absence at a meeting
*   a person's height
*   the number of people at a rugby match
*   a deadline for returning a machine on hire
*   the population of the UK
*   someone's name
*   The percentage swings at an election..

2   Write VBA statements for the following:

a) Declare a Long integer variable called *NoOfStars*. Assign the value of 65,000 to this variable.

b) Declare a Single variable called *HeightOfStudent*, and then assign the value of the variable to 1.655.

c) Declare a Currency variable called *PriceOfBook*, and then assign the value of the variable to 18.95.

3   Write a VBA program that will input two numbers using the InputBox function and output the smallest number input using a MsgBox function. Test the program with a suitable range of values.

4   Write a VBA program that will input three values using the InputBox function, and output in a blank sheet using the cell range C2:C4, the three numbers in reverse order.

5   Consider the following real-world entities and represent them with user defined types as in the examples *EmployeeRecord* and *Course* above: a member/customer of a video shop, a bank account, a book in the library, a CD in a music shop stock system. You will have to decide on which fields are needed for each of the entities. Write an example macro to use one of your user-defined types.

6   Study the following code and see if you can work out what it does. Then open the *weeklySales* worksheet of the SALESMAN workbook, go to the VBE and enter this sub procedure. Run and test using suitable values.

```
Sub listBonusValues()
    Dim bonus(12) As Currency    'declare 3 variables as integers
    Dim bonus_number As Currency
    Dim index As Integer
    Dim cell As Object
    Dim strMsg As String
    bonus_number = InputBox(prompt:="enter bonus value")
        'ask the user for some values
    index = 0
    For Each cell In Range("month_bonus")
        bonus(index) = cell.Value
        index = index + 1
    Next
    strMsg = "Current bonuses of salesmen: &vbCr &vbCr"
    For index = 0 To 8
        strMsg = strMsg & Str(bonus(index)) & vbCr
    Next
    MsgBox strMsg, vbOKOnly + vbInformation, "Array of bonuses"
End Sub
```

7   Create a new workbook called *my_array_book*. Write a VBA macro that declares an array called *MyArray* of size 8. Input the array items using the **InputBox** function. Under the headings 'Array elements' and 'Array reverse elements' the macro should transfer the array to column A in the default worksheet. The program should also write the contents of the array in reverse order to column B of the worksheet. (Hint: to write the contents in reverse use **For num =8 to 1 step –1**).

6 Decisions in VBA

Comparison operators 114

Comparing different data types .. 116

Logical operators 122

Select case 123

The operators in VBA 127

Exercises 128

Comparison operators

Computers do more than calculate – among other things they also make decisions. VBA macros can select a course of action that depends on the outcome of some decision. We have already encountered one way in which this can be done by using the **If … Then** statements. This chapter will look at VBA decision-making statements in a little more detail.

When we used a statement like **If cell.Value > 0 Then** in previous chapters, the expression **cell.Value** has to be greater than 0 before the result will succeed. In other words, the result of the comparison must be true. This is called a *comparison operator*. Clearly, the comparison operators produce Boolean outcomes, because the outcome of the comparison is either true or false. The mathematical operators, discussed in previous chapters, produce numeric values, whereas the comparison operators produce Boolean results. Table 6.1 gives some illustrations of comparison operators.

Table 6.1 Some comparison operators used in VBA

Operator	Example of use	Description
>	This > that	The greater than operator returns True if the value on the left side of > is numerically or alphabetically greater than the value on the right.
<	bonus < 2000.00	The less than operator returns True if the value on the left side of < is numerically or alphabetically less than the value on the right.
= *or* Is	Rng Is Nothing	The Is operator (used to compare two object references) returns True if the object Rng is the same as the Nothing range.
>=	FirstName >= "Mike"	The greater than or equal to operator returns True if the value on the left side of >= is numerically or alphabetically greater than or equal to the value on the right.
<=	Num <= cell.Value	The less than or equal to operator returns True if the value on the left side of <= is numerically or alphabetically less than or equal to the value on the right.
<>	Range("D1") <> "Amy"	The not equal to operator returns True if the value on the left side of <> is numerically or alphabetically unequal to the value on the right.

String comparisons

When you compare strings, VBA uses the American Standard Code for Information Interchange (ASCII) codes, to determine how to compare the characters. For example, the ASCII code for the uppercase letter A – whose ASCII code is 65 – is less than the uppercase letter B (ASCII code 66). The ASCII codes for the lower case characters are the same for the Uppercase characters plus 32. Hence, the ASCII code for lowercase 'a' is $65 + 32 = 97$, the ASCII code for lowercase 'b' is $66 + 32 = 98$, and so on. To use comparison operators in your programs, you must understand how they get their true or false results. The If statement, introduced in the next section, explains how you can use these results to make decisions in your program. Before you read the next section, make sure that you understand how these operators compare values.

Table 6.2 Examples of comparison operators

Relation	Result
4 > 1	True
4 < 1	False
4 < 8	True
"straw" <= "wood"	False
"Keith Darlington" < "keith darlington"	True
0 >= 0	True
0 <= 0	True
1 <> "one"	True
2 >= 3	False

Self-assessment exercise

Which of the following inequalities produce true results?

a) $100.0 = 100.000$

b) "Tony Blair" > "Gordon Brown"

c) $5 < 1$

d) "Manic Street Preachers" <> "manic street preachers"

Comparing different data types

The expressions on both sides of a comparison operator must conform to the same data type or at least compatible data types. You cannot compare a string to a numeric data type, e.g. "one" with 1. They are stored differently in the computer, and if you try, you will get a type mismatch error. You can compare any numeric data type against any other numeric data type most of the time. In other words, you can test whether a single-precision value is less than or greater than an integer value, such as **100 >99.99**. Clearly, this comparison would return the result *True*.

The If statements

Many of the previous examples have shown that programs often have to make decisions. This means that a program will follow one course of action if one comparison is true or perhaps another course of action if it is false. There are two main structures for implementing decisions in VBA: **If** and **Select Case**.

If uses the comparison operators you learned earlier in this lesson to test data values, and can test whether to execute complete blocks of code. This means that If lets your program execute only parts of the program if the data warrants partial execution. In this section we will look at three variants of the If statement. These are:

- ◆ One-way selection using **If...Then**
- ◆ Two-way selection using **If...Then...Else**
- ◆ Multiway selection using **If...Then......ElseIf...Else**

The one-way If structure: If...Then

The one-way **If** structure is used in programs when some course of action is taken if the outcome of a decision is true; otherwise, no alternative action is taken when the decision is false. It has the following syntax:

```
If ComparisonTest Then
    one or more VBA statements
End If
```

The **End If** statement lets VBA know where the body of the **If** structure ends.

Suppose we wanted to write a macro that prompts the user with an InputBox to enter a range of cells, which it will then highlight. The program is implemented in Listing 6.1. It uses a one-way **If…Then** statement, that checks to see if that the range variable *Rng* is not empty. If it is not, then the range is selected using the **Rng.Select** statement.

Listing 6.1

```
'Highlights selected user range
Sub GetRange()
    Dim Rng As Range
    Set Rng = Application.InputBox (prompt: = "Enter range", Type: =8)
    If Not (Rng Is Nothing) Then
        Rng.Select
    End If
End Sub
```

Figure 6.1 Screenshot from Listing 6.1

Tip

Be careful when you compare non-integers for equality. Decimal numbers are difficult to represent internally. For example, if you assigned 10.2342 to a single-precision variable and assigned 10.2342 to a double-precision variable, VBA might return false if you compare the values for equality. Internally, one of the variables might actually hold 10.32420001 because of rounding errors when storing significant figures. You can safely compare two currency values for equality, however, because VBA compares their accuracy to two decimal places.

The two-way If

The one-way **If** statement is applied when you want the program to execute one set of instructions if some condition is true, otherwise do nothing. However, you may want the program to execute one set of instructions if some condition is true, else execute another set of instructions. This type of logical construct is called a two way if statement. The general syntax is:

```
If ComparisonTest Then
    One or more VBA statements
Else
    One or more VBA statements
End If
```

We can see that whereas **If** executes code based on the comparison test's true result, the **Else** statement executes code based on the comparison test's false result. **Else** is an optional part of the **If** statement and specifies the code that executes if the comparison test is false.

If we look at the previous example, we can see that there is a problem. If a valid range is selected then the range is highlighted, if not, then nothing happens. However, in this event, we might want to prompt the user to enter a valid range, perhaps using a **MsgBox**. A two-way **If** structure has been used to implement this change in Listing 6.2. Note that the comparison test is the same, but an **Else** alternative displays the error message (see Figure 6.2).

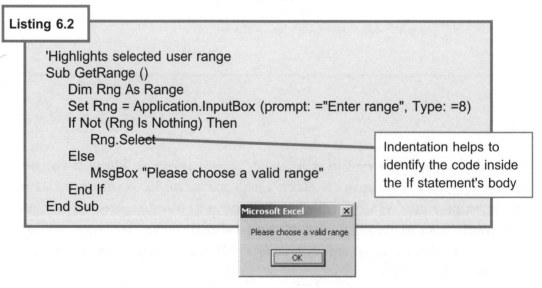

Listing 6.2

```
'Highlights selected user range
Sub GetRange ()
    Dim Rng As Range
    Set Rng = Application.InputBox (prompt: ="Enter range", Type: =8)
    If Not (Rng Is Nothing) Then
        Rng.Select
    Else
        MsgBox "Please choose a valid range"
    End If
End Sub
```

Indentation helps to identify the code inside the If statement's body

Microsoft Excel

Please choose a valid range

OK

Figure 6.2 The error message from Listing 6.2

118

This next example shows how the two-way **If** can be used. This macro will input a person's sex and display the message "You can retire at 60" if the sex of the person is female, otherwise display the message "You can retire at the age of 65". It uses a string variable to store the sex of the person, which is input through an **InputBox** command. The two-way **If** then checks if the sex is female and outputs the corresponding message. Otherwise, it displays the alternative message.

Listing 6.3 Another two-way If example

```
Sub retireAge ()
Dim sex As String
sex = InputBox ("Input the sex of the person", "Person's Sex")
If (sex="female")
    Then MsgBox "You can retire at the age of 60"
Else
    MsgBox "You can retire at 65"
End Sub
```

Parentheses are not required around the test but they help separate it from the rest of the code

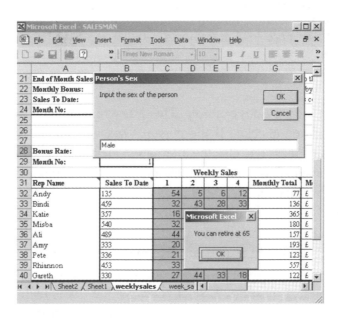

Figure 6.3 Screenshot from Listing 6.3

Self-assessment exercise

What is wrong with this **If** statement?

```
If (z > 0) Then
    MsgBox "This"
Else
    MsgBox "That"
End Else
```

The multi-way If statement

The two-way **If** statement is applied when you want the program code to execute one set of instructions if some condition is true, else execute another set of instructions. However, there are times when you may want to execute one set of instructions if some condition is true, or else if some other condition is true, you may want to execute another set of instructions, and so on, until all alternatives have been completed. The general syntax is:

```
If ComparisonTest Then
    One or more VBA statements
Else If
    One or more VBA statements
Else If
    One or more VBA statements
Else
    One or more VBA statements
End If
```

Consider the previous example. This was written as a two-way **If**, where the first condition checked if the person's sex was female and displayed the appropriate message, else the alternative message for a male person would be displayed. The problem is that the program would take any alternative value other than female. We will extend this two-way **If** to a three-way **If** so that first condition will check if the person's sex is female and display the appropriate message, else if the person's sex is male, it will display the male message, else it will display an error message such as "You have entered an invalid sex". In Listing 6.4, the **If** checks if the sex is female and display the corresponding message. **Else If** checks if the sex is male, will display the corresponding, and the final **Else** will display an error message.

Listing 6.4

```
Sub retire_age ()
Dim sex As String
Sex = InputBox ("Input the sex of the person (male or female)", "Person's Sex")
If (sex="female") Then
    MsgBox "You can retire at the age of 60"
Else If (sex = "male") Then
    MsgBox "You can retire at 65"
Else
    MsgBox " Error! You have entered an invalid sex."
End If
End Sub
```

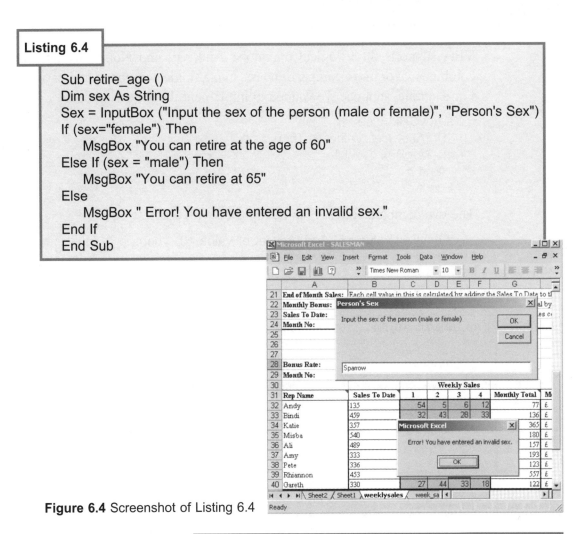

Figure 6.4 Screenshot of Listing 6.4

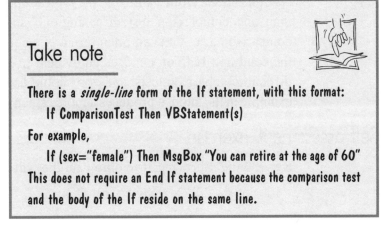

Take note

There is a *single-line* form of the If statement, with this format:

　　If ComparisonTest Then VBStatement(s)

For example,

　　If (sex="female") Then MsgBox "You can retire at the age of 60"

This does not require an End If statement because the comparison test and the body of the If reside on the same line.

Logical operators

VBA supports three logical operators: And, Or, and Not. They let you combine two or more comparison tests into a single compound comparison. For example, suppose we wanted to implement the following code:

```
If (myCell.Value =6) Then
   If (Activecell.Value>0) Then
      MsgBox "Done"
   End If
End If
```

The two comparison tests can be replaced with one test as:

```
If (myCell.Value =6) And (ActiveCell.value >0) Then...
```

Table 6.3 The logical operators

Operator	Example Usage	Description
And	If (myCell.Value=6) And (z<0)	Succeeds, or produces True, if both sides of the And are true. In this example *myCell.Value* must be 6 **And** z must be less than 0. Otherwise, the expression fails.
Or	If (myCell.Value=6) Or (z<0)	Produces True if either side of the Or is true – in this example *myCell.Value* must be 6 **Or** z must be less than 0. Otherwise, the expression produces false.
Not	If (Not x=5)	Negates the result, turning true to false and vice versa. In this condition checks to see if x is not = 5.
If Not	If Not IsNumeric(cell)	For this example, **if** the cell is **not** numeric the true result is returned, else the result is false.

As you can see from Table 6.3, the logical operators let you combine more than one comparison test in a single If statement. The Not negates a comparison test. You can often turn a Not condition around. For example, the condition **If (Not x = 5)** is equivalent to **If (x <> 5)**. Not can produce difficult comparison tests, and you should use it cautiously. In the second example in the table, it produces a more effective result than the alternatives.

Self-assessment exercise

Rewrite the following **If** to eliminate the **Not** and to clarify the code:

```
If Not(x < 20) Or Not(y >= 20) Then
```

Select case

Consider the **If** structure shown in Listing 6.5. Although the logic is simple, the coding is a little difficult to follow.

Listing 6.5 TicketPrice VBA Program

```
If (ticketPrice =20) Then
    MsgBox "Standing at rear"
Else
    If (ticketPrice =30) Then
        MsgBox "Front wing seats"
    Else
        If (ticketPrice =40) Then
            MsgBox "Lower front wing seats"
        Else
            If (ticketPrice =50) Then
                MsgBox " Balcony"
            Else
                If (ticketPrice =60) Then
                    MsgBox "Upper Balcony"
                Else
                    MsgBox "Royal Box"
                End If
            End If
        End If
    End If
End If
```

VBA supports the **Select Case** statement that can make it easier to understand, multiple-choice conditions than **If...ElseIf...Else** statements. The syntax of the **Select Case** statement is as follows:

```
Select Case Expression
    Case value
        one or more VBA statements
    Case value
        one or more VBA statements
    Case value
        one or more VBA statements
    Case Else
        one or more VBA statements
End Select
```

Listing 6.6 is a **Select Case** version of Listing 6.5. **Select Case** organises the multiple-choice selections into a more manageable format.

Listing 6.6 Using Select Case to simplify complex If…Else statements

```
Sub ticketSelect()
Dim ticketPrice As Integer
ticketPrice = InputBox("Input ticket price")
Select Case ticketPrice
  Case 20:  MsgBox "Standing at rear"
  Case 30:  MsgBox "Front wing seats"
  Case 40:  MsgBox "Front lower wing seats"
  Case 50:  MsgBox "Balcony"
  Case 60:  MsgBox "Upper Balcony"
  Case Else:  MsgBox "Royal Box"
End Select
End Sub
```

In this example, if *ticketPrice* holds 20, the message "Standing at rear" is displayed. If it holds 30, "Front wing seats" is displayed. The logic continues through the **Case 60:** statement. If *ticketPrice* holds a value that does not fall in the range 20 to 60, the final **Case Else** displays the message "Royal Box".

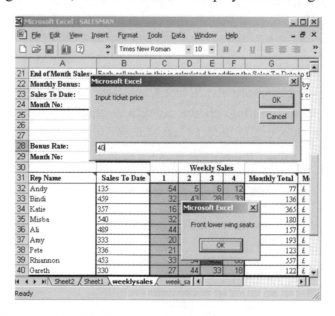

Figure 6.5 Screenshot of Select Case example

The body of each **Case** can consist of more than one statement, just as the body of an **If** or **If...Else** can consist of more than one. VBA executes all the statements for any given **Case** match until the next **Case** is reached. Once VBA executes a matching **Case** value, it skips the remaining **Case** statements and continues with the code that follows **End Select**.

Notice the colons after each **Case** value statement. These are optional, but do help to separate the case being tested from the code that it executes.

Alternative select case formats

You can use variations on the above **Case Select** format as the following syntax shows:

```
Select Case Expression
  Case expr1a To expr2a:
    One or more VBA statements
  Case expr1b To expr2b:
    One or more VBA statements
  Case expr1c To expr2c:
    One or more VBA statements
  Case Else:
    One or more VBA statements
End Select
```

The **Case** lines require a range, such as **4 To 6.** The **To** option enables you to match against a range instead of a relation or an exact match.

Notes on select case

The format of **Select Case** makes it look as difficult as a complex nested **If...Else**, but **Select Case** structures are easier to code and to maintain than their **If...Else** counterparts. **Select Case** is a good substitute for long, nested **If...Else** conditions when several choices are possible.

The Case *expression* can be any VBA expression – such as a calculation, a string value, or a numeric value – provided that it results in an integer or a string value, and this must match the expression's data type.

The **Select Case** structure is useful when you must make several choices based on data values. It can have two or more **Case** *value* sections, and the code that is executed depends on which value matches the expression. You can write an (optional) **Case Else** body of code which will be executed if none of the values match. Otherwise, nothing happens and control continues with the statement that follows **End Select**.

Here is an example of a macro based on *month_bonus* range in the *weeklysales* worksheet of the SALESMAN.XLS workbook The purpose of the macro is to classify cells in the range *weekTotal* by assigning different colours to the cells depending on whether the cell value is less than 60, equal to 60, 61 to 70 or greater than 70. The colours then assigned would be green, red, blue and yellow respectively. In this example (Listing 6.7), we can see that the **Select Case** statement is used for this four-way selection.

Listing 6.7 Implementing a multi-way If using Select Case

```
            Sub HighlightRanges ()
        Dim myCell As Object
          For Each myCell In Range ("weekTotal")
           Select Case myCell.Value
             Case Is < 60
                 myCell.Interior.ColorIndex = 4 'green
             Case Is = 60
                 myCell.Interior.ColorIndex = 3 'red
             Case 61 To 70
                 myCell.Interior.ColorIndex = 5 'blue
             Case Is > 60
                 myCell.Interior.ColorIndex = 6 'yellow
           End Select
         Next
       End Sub
```

Tip

Avoid using Select Case when a simple If or If...Else will do the job. Unless you need to compare against more than a couple of values, use If and If...Else statements because of their simplicity. Use Select Case instead of the embedded If...Else when you have three or more options, because it keeps the code much simpler and easier to maintain.

The operators in VBA

Table 6.4 indicates the symbols that are used for operators in VBA. These have been classified into three groups: Arithmetic, Comparison and Logical operators.

Table 6.4 Operators in VBA

Arithmetic	Comparison	Logical
Exponentiation (^)	Equality (=)	Not
Negation (-)	Inequality (<>)	And
Multiplication and division (*, /)	Less than (<)	Or
Integer division (\)	Greater than (>)	Xor
Modulus arithmetic (Mod)	Less than or equal to (<=)	Eqv
Addition and subtraction (+, -)	Greater than or equal to (>=)	Imp
String concatenation (&)	Like, Is	

Exercises

1   Write a macro that will prompt the user to input a person's name using an **InputBox** and output the message "TooLong" if the name is longer than 30 characters, otherwise the macro should output the message "Name OK".

2   Open a new workbook using the default *sheet1*. Using the cell range C3:C12 enter the following numeric data that represents student examination marks out of 100: 41, 55, 36, 59, 70, 67, 37, 69, 13, 62. Design a VBA macro using structured English pseudocode that will count the number of marks in each category as Distinctions (>=70), Credits (>=60 and < 70) Passes (>=40 and <60) and Failures (<40). From the pseudocode write the VBA macro using the **Select Case** to implement this program. Output the number in each of these categories using the cells E3: H3 under suitable headings.

3   Open a new workbook and enter the table of data shown below into the cell range A2:J3 into sheet1:

Orange	Apple	Apple	Orange	Pear	Apple	Lemon	Orange	Pear	Lemon
Lemon	Orange	Pears	Orange	Orange	Lemon	Orange	Orange	Apple	Apple

Write two separate VBA programs, one that uses multi-way If and the other that uses **Select Case** statements so that the cell colour is orange if the cell value is "Orange", yellow if the cell value is "Lemon", green if the cell value is "Apple" and blue if the cell value is "Pear".

4   Design a macro called *categoriseMonthSales* using structured English for the following task. It should check the value for:

below 0 and 200 then colour the cell green (colorIndex = 31),

between 201 and 500 colour the cell yellow (colorIndex=31),

501 to 1000 colour the cell blue (colorIndex=5),

above 1001, colour the cell another colour (colorIndex=3).

7 Loops

For Each ... Next 130

For... Next loops 132

Exiting a For loop 137

Do ... Loop 139

Loop termination 143

Which loop structure is best? 144

Exercises 145

For Each ... Next

Use this structure when it is required to process all objects in a collection, such as loop around a range of cells in a worksheet. The loop will execute for as many times as there are elements in a specified group, e.g. each worksheet in a workbook, or each cell in a range.

The **For Each ... Next** loop has the basic syntax:

```
For Each element In group
    Statements
Next

For Each cell In Range(range_name)
    Statements
Next
```

In this example the examination mark data shown on the worksheet in Figure 7.1 is analysed so that the number of distinctions (70 or more), credits (50 or more but less than 70) and failures (less than 50) is displayed for each gender in the positions shown. That is, the numbers in the ranges E9:G9 and E16:G16. The procedure, *checkGenderProportions*, has been designed by using a **For ... Next** loop which checks each cell in the range C6:C19 – the ones that contain examination marks. During each repetition of the **For** loop, the cell is checked to see which category it falls into. You can see that the first **If** condition checks to see if the cell value is both female and a distinction, if it is, then the integer variable *female_distinction_count* is incremented. The same testing process is applied to each of the other categories. After the **For... Next** loop has been completed, the categories are output.

Listing 7.1 Examination marks categorisation

```
Sub checkGenderProportions()
    Dim cell As Object
    Dim female_distinction_count As Integer      'counter of female distinction
    Dim female_credit_count As Integer           'counter of female credit
    Dim female_fail_count As Integer             'counter of female failed
    Dim male_distinction_count As Integer        'counter of male distinction
    Dim male_credit_count As Integer             'counter of male credit
    Dim male_fail_count As Integer               'counter of male failed
    For Each cell In Range("c6:c19")
        If (cell. Value = "f") And (cell. Offset (0, -1).Value >= 70) Then
            female_distinction_count = female_distinction_count + 1
```

```
        ElseIf (cell.Value = "f") And (cell.Offset(0, -1).Value >= 50) Then
            female_credit_count = female_credit_count + 1
        ElseIf (cell.Value = "f") And (cell.Offset(0, -1).Value < 50) Then
            female_fail_count = female_fail_count + 1
        End If
        If (cell.Value = "m") And (cell.Offset(0, -1).Value >= 70) Then
            male_distinction_count = male_distinction_count + 1
        ElseIf (cell.Value = "m") And (cell.Offset(0, -1).Value >= 50) Then
            male_credit_count = male_credit_count + 1
        ElseIf (cell.Value = "m") And (cell.Offset(0, -1).Value < 50) Then
            male_fail_count = male_fail_count + 1
        End If
    Next
    Range("e9").Value = female_distinction_count
    Range("f9").Value = female_credit_count
    Range("g9").Value = female_fail_count
    Range("e16").Value = male_distinction_count
    Range("f16").Value = male_credit_count
    Range("g16").Value = male_fail_count
End Sub
```

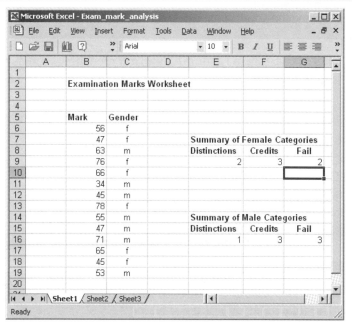

Figure 7.1 The output format for gender categorisation of marks

131

For... Next loops

Loops controlled by a number

The previous example used a **For ...Next** loop to go through all the cells in a range – this is a very powerful way to process spreadsheets. You can also use a number to control how many times a **For ...Next** loop executed. This kind of loop is very common in traditional programming languages when general variables are used. For example, the weekly sales data in the SALESMAN workbook might require calculations to find the total weekly mileage from seven daily totals. Rather than do this manually, a macro could be written whose purpose is to provide an input box for the user to enter the number of sales recorded for a salesman for each day for seven days of the week, add them up and display the total in a message box (see Figure 7.2). In structured English, the program might look like this:

```
Get Daily Sales
    set the totalSales to zero
    For dayCount = 1 To 7
        get the sales for day dayCount
        add this sales to totalSales
    Next day value
    return the totalSales
End
```

The macro is written in Listing 7.2 and a screenshot taken during the program run is shown in Figure 7.3.

Listing 7.2

```
Sub getDailySales()
    Dim totalSales As Integer
    Dim thisDaySales As Variant
    Dim dayCount As Integer
    totalSales = 0
    For dayCount = 1 To 7
        thisDaySales = InputBox(prompt:="enter sales for day: " & dayCount)
        totalSales = totalSales + thisDaySales
    Next
    strTotalSales = str(totalSales)
    MsgBox "The total sales over the 7 days are=" + strTotalSales
End Sub
```

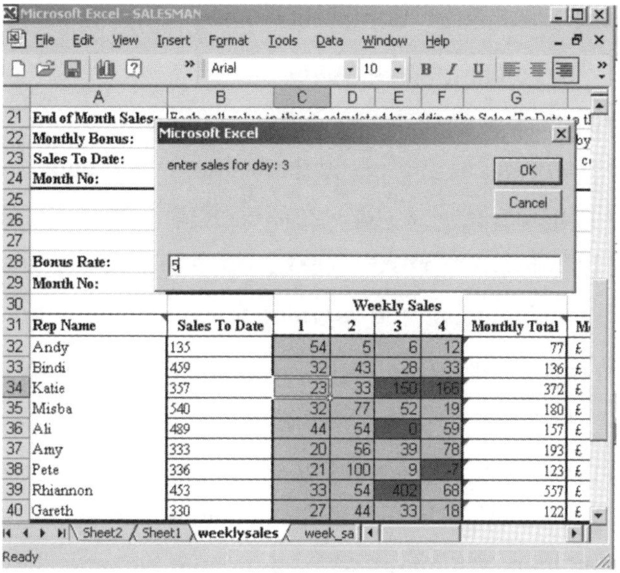

Figure 7.2 Screenshot during run of Listing 7.2

Figure 7.2 shows the output from this program. Notice that during the run each day's sales is input using a separate **InputBox**. The program output total is then included in the Active Cell as well as a **MsgBox** telling the user the total of the 7 days' sales.

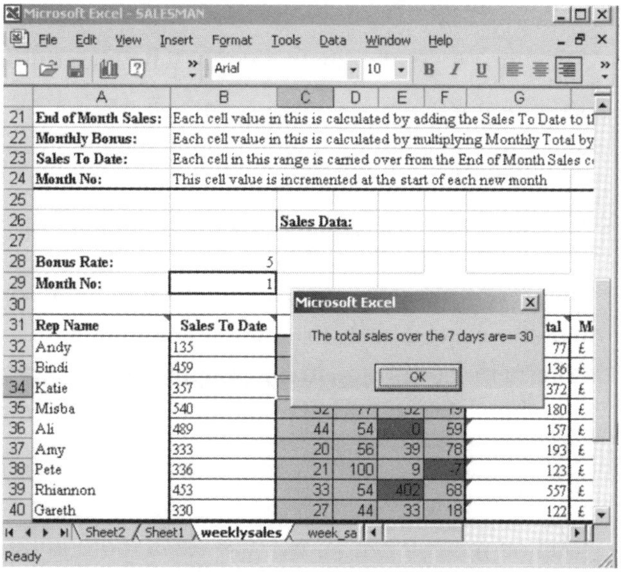

Figure 7.3 MsgBox output on Excel weeksales sheet

The **For... Next** loop in this example works using a counter. The counter:

- has a name – *dayCount*
- starts at a particular value, in this case 1
- terminates at a particular value, in this case 7
- increases by a step value each time through the loop, in this case +1

This form of a **For... Next** loop, has the general syntax:

For *count* = *lowerValue* to *upperValue* Step *stepValue*

Where *lowerValue*, *upperValue* and *stepValue* are all integers. For example:

For count = 3 to 15 step 3

In this loop, the *lowerValue* =3, *upperValue* =15 and *stepValue* =3. This means that the loop will be executed with values of *count* of 3, 6, 9,12, 15.

The loop terminates when the *count* becomes larger than the *upperValue*. There's an exception to this: If you code a negative *stepValue*, the loop terminates when the *count* becomes smaller than the *upperValue*. If you specify a negative *stepValue*, *upperValue* must be less than *lowerValue* or VBA will execute the loop only once.

Self-assessment exercise

State the range of values of count when the following loops when executed:

1   For count = 20 to 10 step -2.

2   For count = 5 to 25 step 5.

Using active cells and jumping around in a For... Next loop

This example uses the *weeklysales* worksheet of the SALESMAN.XLS workbook, to check to see if a salesperson is worthy of promotion. The criteria for promotion in the organisation are currently that the sales person's monthly sales should exceed 1000 units. The macro is given in Listing 7.3.

Active cells are used to implement this program. It is a slightly different approach to what we have seen so far because instead of using a **For... Next** loop on the cell range, we will use a loop on the range of sales staff. To do this, we start with the first active cell in the range then use the **Offset** method

Listing 7.3

```
1  Sub checkPromotion()
2     Application.ScreenUpdating = False
3     Const Promotion As Long = 1000
4     Const MaxSalesman As Integer = 9
5     Dim Count As Integer
6     Worksheets("Weeklysales").Select
7     Range("End_month_sales").Select
8     For Count = 1 To MaxSalesman
9        If ActiveCell.Value > Promotion Then
10          ActiveCell.Interior.ColorIndex = 5
11       End If
12       ActiveCell.Offset(1,0).Select
13    Next
14 End Sub
```

to go to the next cell in the loop. When using active cells, the screen can sometimes jump around when you run the program. To circumvent this, you can freeze the screen while the macro runs by using the code in Line 2, i.e.

    Application.ScreenUpdating = False

This line will ensure that the screen remains frozen until you either assign the property of the value to True, or when your macro finishes execution. You will not have to restore it to true, unless you want to display screen changes while the macro is still running.

After Line 2, some variables are declared, as well as constants set for the *MaxSalesman*, currently 9, and the amount of units sold which would qualify for promotion, currently 1000. Remember that the purpose of the procedure is to check if a salesperson's sales are high enough to be considered for promotion.

Line 5 defines *count* as an integer variable, and line 6 selects the worksheet called *weeklysales*.

Line 7 selects the range of cells called *end_month_sales*. The first cell in this range will then become active.

Line 8 uses a **For... Next** to go through the loop 9 times (i.e. the value of MaxSalesman).

Lines 9–11 check for the promotion condition.

Line 12 uses the Offset method applied to the active cell (i.e. the new active cell becomes the next cell in the range).

The output is shown in Figure 7.4.

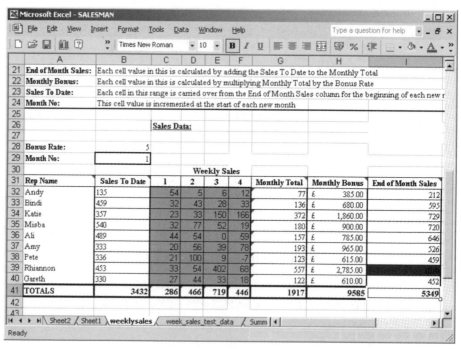

Figure 7.4 Screenshot for Listing 7.3

Exiting a For loop

Sometimes, it is necessary to exit a **For** loop prematurely. For example, if the purpose of the code is to check for a particular value in a **For** range, and that value has been found, then the code should not have to check all other values in that range. However, this will happen because a **For** loop will by default continue through the range. Fortunately, there is a way to circumvent it. You can jump out of the **For... Each** loop when the item has been found by using the **Exit For** statement. The next example illustrates how it works.

Listing 7.4 uses the *weeklySales* sheet from the SALESMAN workbook. This procedure checks each cell in the *rep_name* range to see if a particular name exists, and will output the message "found at" followed by the cell address. It works by declaring a variable called *thisName* that will enable the user to enter a name via an **InputBox**. A Boolean variable *isFound* is use to inform the user whether or not the rep name is found. It does this by initially assuming that it is not found. When the **For...Next** loop begins on Line 8, if the value of *myCell = thisName*, then the rep name has been found and the variable *isFound* is set to True. The MsgBox follows with the appropriate

Listing 7.4

```
1  Sub checkRepName()
2      Dim thisName As Variant
3      Dim myCell As Object
4      Dim isFound As Boolean
5      Worksheets("Weeklysales").Select
6      isFound = False 'assume rep name is not found yet
7      thisName = InputBox(prompt:="enter name")
8      For Each myCell In Range("rep_name")
9        If myCell = thisName Then            'we found it
10           myCell.Interior.ColorIndex = 4
11           isFound = True
12           MsgBox "found at " & myCell.Address
13           Exit For            'jump out of the loop
14       End If
15       Next
16       If Not(isFound) Then
17           MsgBox "The rep name was not found"
18       End If
19  End Sub
```

message. Notice the **Exit For** statement on line 13 – if the *repName* is found then the procedure jumps out of the loop. This means that the **MsgBox** on line 17 will not follow since *isFound* is True. If the rep name is not found, then *isFound* is False so that the MsgBox on Line 17 will then be executed.

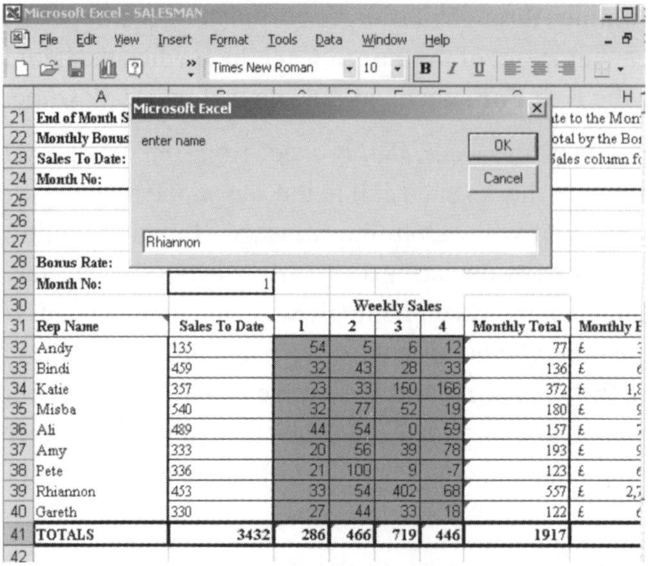

Figure 7.5 Input screenshot for Listing 7.4

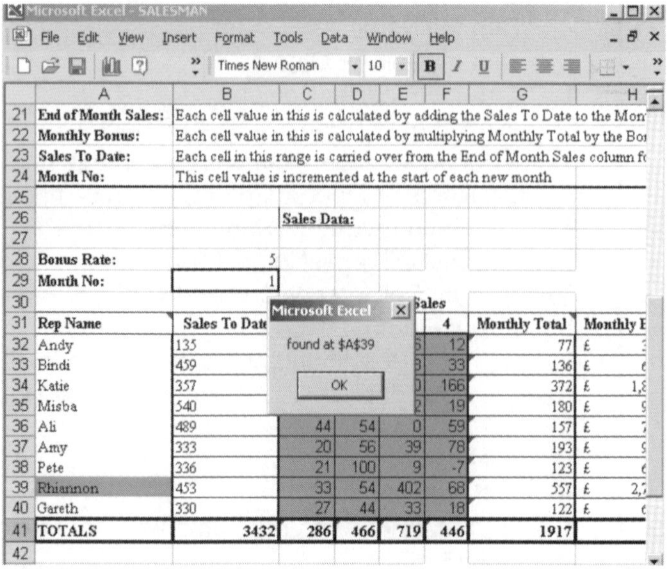

Figure 7.6 Output screenshot for Listing 7.4

Do ... Loop

For loops repeat a fixed number of times that is known in advance. For example, **For count = 1 to 10** will loop exactly 10 times. This is known as *definite iteration*. What happens when we need a program to loop without knowing the number of repetitions in advance? For example, suppose we wanted to create a loop that asked a sales person to input the number of sales during a day. If an unacceptable value, such as a negative number, was input then we would want the program to repeat the prompt until acceptable data was input. The problem is that we don't know in advance how many times it will take before they input an acceptable value. This is known as *indefinite iteration*. The **Do ... Loop** structures allow you to write code that loops an unspecified number of times.

The basic idea about a **Do ...Loop** is that the code in the loop will execute as many times as needed **Until** the test is true, or **While** the test is true. There are four variations of **Do ...Loops** in VBA, which have slight differences in the way they work.

Do Until... Loop

```
Do Until condition
    statements
Loop
```

Example:

```
Do Until sales > 0
    Sales =InputBox (Prompt:="Please input a positive number ")
Loop
```

The condition is applied before entry so the loop may never execute. With an **Until** condition the statements are executed until the condition is true. In the example, the loop will repeat until the user inputs a value >0.

Do While ...Loop

```
Do While condition
    statements
Loop
```

Example:

```
Do While sales <= 0
    Sales =InputBox (Prompt:="Please input a positive number ")
Loop
```

The condition is again applied before entry so the loop may never execute. With a **While** condition, the statements are executed while the condition is true. In this example, the condition has been negated to achieve the same effect as in **Do Until...Loop**.

Do...Loop Until

```
Do
    statements
Loop Until condition
```

Example:

```
Do
    Sales =InputBox (Prompt:="Please input a positive number ")
Loop Until sales > 0
```

The condition is applied *after* the statements and so at least one entry to the loop is guaranteed. Here, the **InputBox** statement will execute at least once. During design stage, think about whether you want this to happen.

Do ...Loop While

```
Do
    statements
Loop While condition
```

Example:

```
Do
    Sales =InputBox (Prompt:="Please input a positive number ")
Loop While sales < 0
```

The condition is again applied after the statements and so at least one entry to the loop is guaranteed. This is the same problem as in **Do ... Loop Until** except that because we are using **While**, we need to negate the condition to achieve the same effect.

Take note

Remember that the comparison test for the Do Until... Loop must be false for the loop to continue.

Using the Do Until...loop

The macro shown in Listing 7.5 enables a sales representative's age to be input and validated in the range 25 to 65. Any value outside this range is rejected by the macro, and the user is forced to re-input again. The macro continues to loop until the user has entered acceptable data.

Listing 7.5 Using Do...Until to control a loop

```
Sub ageDoUntil()
   Dim strAge As String
   Dim intAge As Integer
   strAge = InputBox("How old are you?", "Age Ask")
      'Get the age in a string variable
   If (strAge = "") Then End
      'Check for the Cancel command button, if so, terminate the program
   intAge = Val(strAge)
      'Cancel was not pressed, so convert Age to integer
   Do Until ((intAge >= 25) And (intAge <= 65))
         'Loop if the age is not in the correct range
      MsgBox("Your age must be between 25 and 65", vbExclamation, "Error!")
         'The salesman's age is out of range
      strAge = InputBox("How old are you?", "Age Ask")
      If (strAge = "") Then End
         'Terminate the program when Cancel button pressed
      intAge = Val(strAge)
   Loop
End Sub
```

The Listing uses the built-in **Val()** function. **Val()** accepts a string argument and converts that string to a number (assuming that the string holds the correct digits for a number). The **InputBox** function returns a string so the value that the user enters into the input box must convert to an integer before you store the value in the integer variable named intAge.

The **Do Until ((intAge >= 25) And (intAge <= 65))** loops until the user enters a value that's more than or equal to 25 and less than or equal to 65.

141

Do While ... Loop

Do While... Loop works in almost exactly the same way as **Do Until... Loop** like except that the **Until** variation continues executing the body of the loop until the comparison test is true. Here is the format of the **Do While... Loop** structure:

```
Do While (comparison test)
    block of one or more VBA statements
Loop
```

The block of code continues looping as long as comparison test is true. Whether you insert one or several lines of code for the block doesn't matter. It's vital, however, that the block of code somehow changes a variable used in the comparison test. The block of code keeps repeating as long as the **Do While... Loop**'s comparison test continues to stay true. Eventually, the comparison test must become false or your program will enter an infinite loop and the user will have to break the program's execution through an inelegant means, such as pressing the **[Ctrl] + [Break]** key combination.

Do While... Loop continues executing a block of VBA statements as long as the comparison test is true. As soon as comparison test becomes false, the loop terminates.

Tip

An infinite loop is a loop that never terminates. Guard against infinite loops and always make sure your loops can terminate properly. Even if you provide an Exit command button or a File > Exit menu option in your application, the program will often ignore the user's exit command if the program enters an infinite loop.

Loop termination

As long as the comparison test is true, the block of code in the body of the loop continues executing. When the test becomes false, the loop terminates and VBA begins program execution at the statement following the **Loop** statement which signals the end of the loop. As soon as the **Do While**'s comparison test becomes false, the loop terminates and doesn't execute even one more time. The test appears at the top of the loop, so if it is false the first time the loop begins, the body of the loop will never execute.

Listing 7.6 contains the same program as in Listing 7. 5 using a **Do While ... Loop** to asks the user for an age. If the user enters an age less than 25 or more than 65, the program returns an error message as before. It continues looping, asking for the age, as long as the user enters an age that's out of range.

Listing 7.6 Using Do While loop to control a loop

```
Dim strAge As String
Dim intAge As Integer
Dim intPress As Integer        'Get the age in a string variable
strAge = InputBox("How old are you?", "Age Ask")
' Check for the Cancel command button
If (strAge = "") Then
    End                              'Terminates the application
End If
    'Cancel was not pressed, so convert age to integer using Val()
intAge = Val(strAge)
    'Loop if the age is not in the correct range
Do While ((intAge < 25 ) Or (intAge > 65))
'The user's age is out of range
    intPress = MsgBox("Your age must be between " & _
        "10 and 65", vbExclamation, "Error!")
    strAge = InputBox("How old are you?", "Age Ask")
        'Check for the Cancel command button
    If (strAge = "") Then
        End                          'Terminate the program
    End If
    intAge = Val(strAge)
Loop
```

Which loop structure is best?

As a general rule, it is best to use the loop that makes for the cleanest and clearest comparison test. Sometimes, the logic makes the **Do While** clearer, whereas other loops seem to work better when you set them up with **Do Until**. Remember, **Do Until** continues executing a block of VBA statements as long as the comparison test is false. As soon as the test becomes true, the loop terminates and the program continues on the line that follows the closing **Loop** statement. Remember also, that when the comparison test appears at the bottom of the loop instead of at the top of the loop, the body of the loop will be guaranteed to execute at least one time. Whereas, when the comparison appears at the top of the loop, then depending on the test comparison the loop may not execute even once.

Listing 7.7 is a version of the age-checking program that's much shorter than the previous ones. The comparison test appears at the bottom of the loop, so the extra **InputBox** function call is not needed.

Listing 7.7 Using the Do…Loop While to test at the end of the loop

```
Sub ageDecision()
    Dim strAge As String
    Dim intAge As Integer
    Dim intPress As Integer
    Do
        strAge = InputBox("How old are you?", "Age Ask")
        If (strAge = "") Then      'Check for no data - i.e. the Cancel button
            End                    'Terminate program
        End If
        intAge = Val(strAge)
        If ((intAge < 10) Or (intAge > 99)) Then          'age out of range
            intPress = MsgBox("Your age must be between " & _
            "10 and 99", vbExclamation, "Error!")
        End If
    Loop While ((intAge < 25) Or (intAge > 65))
End Sub
```

Exercises

1   Open the *weeklySales* worksheet of the SALESMAN workbook. Study the following procedure. You will see it is fairly similar to that in Listing 7.4. See if you can see what their differences are. Write and test the procedure.

```
Option Compare Text 'not case sensitive testing
Sub getValidRepName()
    Dim thisRepName As Variant
    Dim myCell As Object
    Dim isFound As Boolean
    Worksheets("Weeklysales").Select
    isFound = False                     'assume repName is not found yet
    Do Until isFound
        thisRepName = InputBox(prompt:="enter a rep name")
        'For loop tries to find this representative name in list
        For Each myCell In Range("Rep_name")
            If myCell = thisRepName Then       'good – it has been found
                myCell.Interior.ColorIndex = 4
                isFound = True
                MsgBox "found at " & myCell.Address
            End If
        Next
    Loop
End Sub
```

2   Open a new workbook. Enter the following values into the range B2 to B6: January, February, March, April and May. Design a VBA program using structured English pseudocode, and from it write a sub procedure that will write the contents of these cells in reverse order in the cells from D2 to D6. (**Hint**: write the contents of the range into an array and then output the array in reverse order in the destination range using **For num = 5 To 1 Step –1**).

3   Open the weeklySales worksheet of the SALESMAN workbook. Go to the VBE and write a VBA procedure that will input from the user, the first two characters of a rep's name and check each cell in the *rep_name* range to see if it contains these letters. If it does, the program should output the message "found" with the corresponding rep name. The program should then continue checking to see if any other names contain the letters and do the same again if other names are found. Run and test your program.

4   Extend the sub procedure that you have written in (2) above by displaying a message box which counts the number of reps whose names begin with the same two first characters.

5   Write two VBA procedures that will prompt the user to input their age as an integer variable. One procedure should then check the value input is less than 120 using a **Do... While** loop. The other procedure should use a **Do... Until** loop. Check to see that your program works correctly using both structures.

Take note

There is really no technical advantage to using Do While or Do Until. Use whichever one seems to flow the best for any given application.

8 Debugging and testing

Types of programming errors ... 148

Testing and debugging 151

The Debug tools 154

The Immediate window 160

Maintenance of VBA programs .. 166

Exercises 167

Types of programming errors

Building a macro and getting it to run isn't the end of the development process. The programmer must ensure the macro does the job it is meant to do. This requires testing and – if the macro doesn't run correctly – fixing the errors (bugs). This is called *debugging*. Sometimes macros will pass the tests, and sometimes they will fail. Test failure is extremely common in a software developer's life irrespective of their skills and experience. It is the exception rather than the rule that a program runs correctly first time. A substantial amount of a software developer's life is spent finding and correcting errors in programs.

Programming errors fall into three categories in VBA. They are syntax errors, run-time errors and logical errors

Syntax errors

All programmers are likely to encounter syntax errors at some time or another. Syntax errors arise during the writing of the code as a result of grammatical, punctuation or spelling mistakes. In VBA, a line containing a syntax error will be shown in red, highlighting the offending word or line item. The programmer must correct the error before the code can be run. An example is shown in Figure 8.1. This syntax error has arisen because the programmer has failed to include a space between the keywords **If** and **Not**.

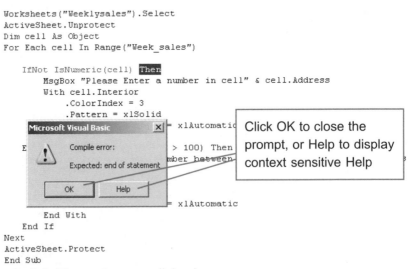

Figure 8.1 The syntax error dialog box

There are many other examples where this type or error could occur. For example, failing to include an end quote when referring to a named range, or making a spelling mistake in a VBA keyword by writing something like 'InputtBox' instead of 'InputBox'. To correct a syntax error, you must know the correct syntax. Use the built-in on-line Help and the line syntax checker to help resolve syntax errors.

Run-time errors

Run-time errors occur during program execution. The sources of these errors are many. For example, attempting to enter an invalid input such as a Currency value instead of an Integer, or to reference an incorrectly named range, or to open a workbook file which does not exist, or even to divide something by zero (0). All of these would precipitate a run-time error. Note that the background colour of the line where the run-time error occurs is yellow. This indicates that the program execution has stopped at that line – called a *line break*.

Normally a run-time error message dialog box would accompany the error, an example of which is shown in Figure 8.2. Note that the dialog box includes four option buttons:

♦ **Continue**. In this example the button is greyed out, meaning that continuing with the run is not an option since the error prevents this from being possible.

♦ The **End** option is not going to help solve the problem, and is there for those who know what the problem is and want to quickly close the dialog box.

♦ **Debug** will display the offending line on a yellow background.

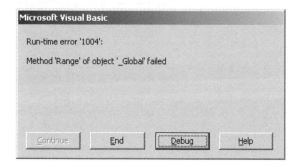

Figure 8.2 An example of a run-time error message dialog box

- Help will give context sensitive Help, though this is generally better suited to experienced programmers because of its technical depth.

Logical errors

Logical errors are not accompanied with error messages, because these errors occur from the program doing something different to that of its intended meaning. In other words, these arise from program semantics. Unfortunately, this is not as easy as it sounds because a program cannot ascertain what a user's intentions were. For example, suppose that a programmer inadvertently used an incorrect formula during the writing of a macro; how would Excel know what the intended formula was? The only way to be sure that a program works properly is to apply a rigorous test and debugging regime. The following section shows how logical errors can be eradicated by using a test and debugging methodology. The test methodology will give confidence in the program correctness, and the debugging methods will provide the facilities to ensure that the job is being done in the correct way.

Tip

When using the VBA Help system, you will often find examples that illustrate concepts. Do read these examples for they will often enhance your understanding of the concept.

Testing and debugging

Testing a macro

When you create a macro, you would normally fix any syntax and run-time errors before debugging begins. Correcting syntax and run-time errors may enable the macro to run but does not guarantee that the program does what it was intended to do. That is, given certain input, does it produce the correct output? Moreover, does it always produce the correct output? A program may appear to do what it is meant to do most of the time, but if it produces the wrong output, even occasionally, then the macro is hardly likely to be acceptable. Hence, test data and a test plan is required that is enough to give confidence in the macro, but not so scrupulous that excessive time is spent on testing.

The black box testing methodology

The black box testing methodology treats the testing process as a 'black box', i.e. the only concern is to know that given certain input(s), then particular output(s) values will be expected (see Figure 8.3). What happens inside the program is ignored: this is why it is called black box testing.

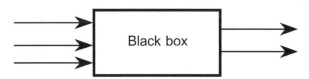

Figure 8.3 Black box diagram

Testing rationale

Clearly, any testing must be such that it is known in advance what the program should do. This means that if certain input data is supplied to the macro, then it should be possible to predict how the macro will perform in terms of output. If it isn't possible to predict how the program will behave with certain input data, then it is clearly not possible to test it! Therefore, any test methodology will require some test data and predictions as to what should happen to it.

The test plan

A range of input data, both valid and invalid, needs to be carefully selected to give confidence in the working of the program. This usually involves creating a table of data to carry out a series of tests to develop enough confidence in the program: the test plan. The first column in the table should refer to the test number. Following columns would list combinations of input data so that all possible paths in the program are going to be tested. The final right-hand column should show the expected result. When you carry out the tests you will need to keep a log of the results: the test log.

The test log

The purpose of the test log is to provide a record of the tests that have been carried out. The test log too should be in tabular format with the same tests used as in the test plan. It should contain columns for the predicted and actual results, as well as the a column displaying the date that the test was conducted. If the results of your test are different from your predictions, then an error has occurred in the program that would have to be fixed. When an error is fixed, all tests that were completed successfully before the erroneous test would have to be repeated, in case fixing the bug causes something to go wrong in another part of the program.

Test evidence

The test log should also include a column linking the actual tests to evidence in the form perhaps, of screen shots or other hard copy evidence proving the tests have been successful. The hard copies of evidence should therefore contain references to test numbers.

Testing a validation program

This example will take the validation program (Listing 4.2) and apply the black box method of testing. Recall that the purpose of this program was to validate the week sales range of data for each sales representative on the *weeklysales* worksheet of the SALESMAN workbook. In this example, data input into each cell had to be numeric, and in the range 0 to 100.

To use the black box method of testing, we first need to decide on ranges for selecting appropriate data. As a starting point, we could consider the input of non-numeric data, such as an alphabetic character. If such a value is input into a cell in the range *week_sales* then we would expect an error message. We could choose an arbitrary character value to test, e.g. 'r'.

If numeric data is input, then there are a number of ranges to consider. Consider first the valid range 0–100, we can choose an arbitrary value in this range, e.g. 44. We also need to choose the boundary points which are 0 and 100, because both these points are valid data points. Then, we need to consider invalid numeric data, e.g. values <0 or >100. Again, if we take arbitrary values like -7 and 3454. This will give 6 tests in total.

Table 8.1 The test plan for the validate program

Test Number	Value of Cell chosen	Predicted Result
1	"r"	Error message and cell colour change
2	44	No change
3	0	No change
4	100	No change
5	-7	Error message and cell colour change
6	3454	Error message and cell colour change

The next step is to produce the test log (Table 8.2). If we analyse it, we can see that there is a problem with Test Number 4 – all other tests are OK at this stage. In the next section we will discuss how to set about fixing errors.

Table 8.2 The test log for the validate program

Test No	Date	Predicted Result	Actual Result
1	18 Nov 02	Error message & cell colour change	Error message & cell colour change
2	18 Nov 02	No change	No change
3	19 Nov 02	No change	No change
4	21 Nov 02	No change	Error message & cell colour change
5	22 Nov 02	Error message & cell colour change	Error message & cell colour change
6	22 Nov 02	Error message & cell colour change	Error message & cell colour change

The Debug tools

The VBE contains some powerful tools for debugging your program. One of the most important of these is the provision of a Watch window combined with the setting of Breakpoints. Figure 8.4 shows the facilities available on the **Debug** toolbar.

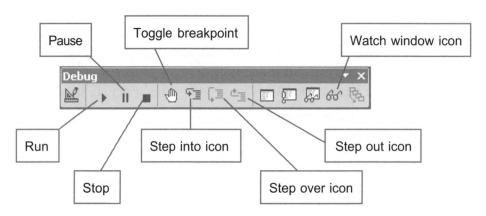

Figure 8.4 The Debug toolbar

The Watch window (the glasses icon)

The Watch window lets you monitor one or more of the variables or cells or whatever as the program runs. Clicking this icon or choosing **Add Watch...** from the **Debug** menu will prompt the user with a dialog box as shown in Figure 8.5. In the case of the *validateWeekSales* program we are interested in watching the range variable *cell*, since this is going to contain the values of the input used in the tests. As you can see in Figure 8.5, this has been entered in the **Expression** box (all other list boxes and radio buttons have been left with the default values unchanged).

Click **OK** and you will see a split horizontal window VBE display (Figure 8.6). Notice that the bottom window (title Watches) is the Watch window, and displays four columns:

♦ The first column displays the name of the expression (i.e. cell).

♦ The second column displays the value. Before running the macro it is shown to be '< Out of Context >' since it does not know what its value is until the program is running.

- The third column displays the type. Again, the current value is *Empty* since a value will not be assigned until the program is running.
- Finally, the fourth column displays the context. The display tells us that the context is *othersalesmanmacros.validateWeekSales*. In other words, this

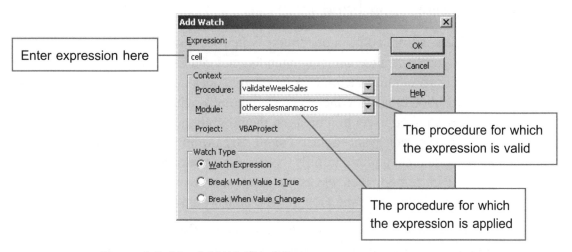

Figure 8.5 The Add Watch window

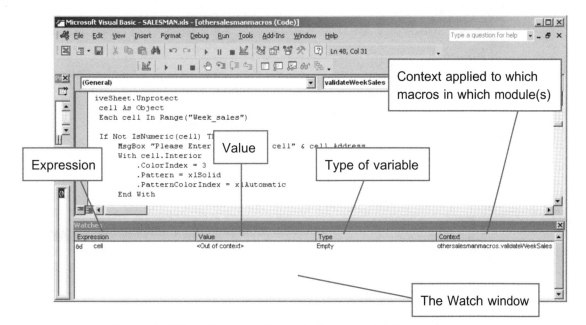

Figure 8.6 The Watches window before running the program

macro is stored in the *othersalesmanmacros* module and is called *validateWeekSales*. Having set the watch we now need to set a breakpoint so that we can pause during each loop execution to see what is happening to the cell.

Toggle Breakpoint: (the hand icon)

There is little point in opening a Watch window, unless you can slow the program operation down enough to get a chance to see what is happening during program execution. A *breakpoint* does exactly that: it sets a program execution break at a line of code as a point at which the program will pause. It is a forced execution break in the program, and you can set breakpoints wherever you want. Select **Toggle Breakpoint** on the **Debug** menu and choose breakpoints carefully, because if, for example, you are **Watch**ing a cell in a loop, then clearly a breakpoint would have to be positioned somewhere inside the loop, otherwise it would not achieve its objective.

To remove the breakpoint, select it and use **Debug > Toggle Breakpoint**.

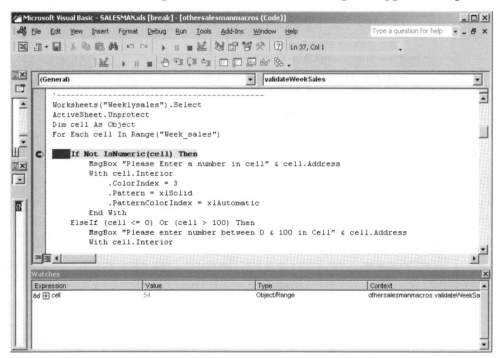

Figure 8.7 The Breakpoint line (With cell.Interior) and the Watch window.

With regard to the *validateWeekSales* macro, a good place to set a breakpoint would be on line **If Not IsNumeric(cell) Then**. This is because this line is inside the loop and therefore will stop during each loop execution. To turn this line into a breakpoint, position the cursor over this line and select **Toggle Breakpoint** from the **Debug** menu. Note that the line will be displayed with a brown background colour, indicating that it is a breakpoint. Figure 8.7 shows the breakpoint line in the VBE module window and the Watch window during the first program loop. Notice that the cell value is 54 as expected.

Tracing

The process of executing one line at a time is known as tracing or code stepping. The VBA debugger provides some facilities relating to tracing. These are: **Step Into**, **Step Over** and **Step Out**.

Step Into

The **Step Into** button on the **Debug** toolbar lets you step through the statements in the procedure one at a time in order to see the sequence in which the statements are executed. Click the **Step Into** button – or use the option on the **Debug** menu – to start, then continue to click **Step Into** to step through the macro. Each time that you click this button the statement that is about to be executed is highlighted.

Step Over

Step Into works by stepping through a program on line at a time in sequence. However, if one sub calls another, then you might want the debugger to step over the called sub. This can be done by using the **Step Over** option. This means that it will execute the called sub all at once, without stepping through it. As an example, consider the two procedures that are named *GetRange* and *CountRange* as shown in Listings 8.1 and 8.2. The purpose of the *GetRange* procedure is to enable the user to enter a cell range, and the procedure would select the cell range on the worksheet. Moreover, the procedure would then call another procedure called *CountRange* whose purpose would be to output to the user the number of cells in the selected range.

To see how this works, if we examine the *GetRange* procedure, we see that the user range is obtained by using a range variable, *Rng*, stored from the **InputBox** function (line 4). Line 5 then checks to see that the user has selected a range using the If statement. If not, then an "Operation Cancelled" message appears, otherwise the selected range is highlighted on the worksheet (line 8), and then on line 9, we can see that the *CountRange* procedure is called. This means that program control will immediately transfer directly to the *CountRange* procedure. At this point, it is said to 'step into' *CountRange* (Listing 8.2), and the **If TypeName(Selection) = "Range" Then** line will be executed, followed by the other lines in the procedure in the sequence. Once this procedure has been completed, control will then return to the *GetRange* procedure to the point following the transfer to *CountRange*, i.e., line 10. If we were to click the **Step Into** button successively during execution, then we would step into each line of both procedures. However, if we were to click the **Step Over** button, then it would 'step over' any called procedures during execution. You might use this option, if you are confident about the called procedures, but wish to debug the main procedure.

Step Out

If you want to discontinue stepping through a sub, you can click **Step Out** which will skip through the remaining steps. You would normally use this when perhaps what you have seen has enabled you to reach a conclusion on the nature of the problem.

Listing 8.1 The calling procedure GetRange

```
1    'Highlights selected range
2    Sub GetRange()
3       Dim Rng As Range
4       Set Rng = Application.InputBox(prompt:="Enter range", Type:=8)
5       If Rng Is Nothing Then
6          MsgBox "Operation Cancelled"
7       Else
8          Rng.Select
9          CountRange
10      End If
11   End Sub
```

Listing 8.2 The called procedure CountRange

```
Sub CountRange()

   If TypeName(Selection) = "Range" Then
       MsgBox Selection.Count
   Else
        MsgBox "N/A"
   End If
End Sub
```

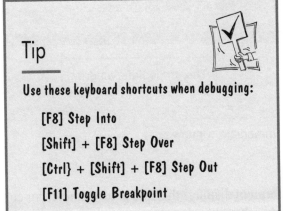

Tip

Use these keyboard shortcuts when debugging:

[F8] Step Into

[Shift] + [F8] Step Over

[Ctrl} + [Shift] + [F8] Step Out

[F11] Toggle Breakpoint

The Immediate window

The Immediate window provides an opportunity to enter a line of code that will execute immediately. It is displayed by default the first time you open the Debug window, otherwise to display it, select **View > Immediate Window** or press **[Crtl] + [G]**. The Immediate window provides an ideal tool for experimentation; for the result of any command entered is immediately interpreted. In the example shown in Figure 8.8, the effect of the command: **ActiveCell.Value = 4** can be seen to be entered immediately in the ActiveCell shown (i.e. C17) This is useful because the Excel Output window can be tiled with the Immediate window.

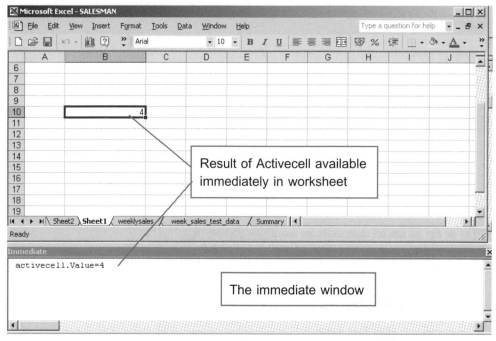

Figure 8.8 Using the Immediate window

Other Debug facilities

The **Debug.Print** statement displays the values of variables, or cells, as they change during execution. The Immediate window is used to display output from **Debug.Print**. To see how this works, suppose we wanted to display the contents of each cell during the running of the *validateWeekSales* macro. We could do this by adding these lines during the loop execution:

```
Debug.Print "The Cell Value is =", cell.Value
```

Figure 8.9 shows how this statement has been added to the *validateWeekSales* procedure. Notice that the statement has been inserted below the start of the **For...Next** loop. The results are displayed in the Immediate window.

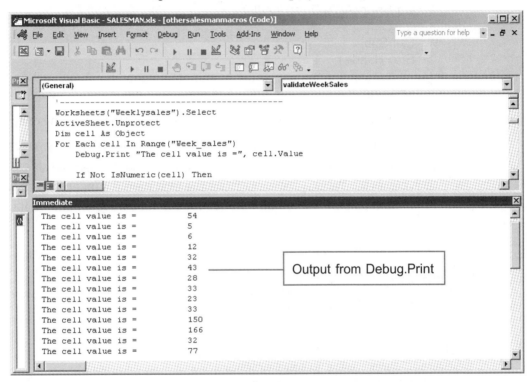

Figure 8.9 Using the Debug.Print statement

Trapping errors

Many programmers make the mistake of assuming that the user will always do what they are expected to do. However, this is a false assumption, for no matter what effort programmers make to provide explanations, users are still liable to carry out erroneous actions. The programmer therefore needs to anticipate user errors and handle them appropriately. The **On Error GoTo** *Label* statement provides one such way of doing this. It tells VBA what to do when a run-time error occurs. When you use an **On Error Goto** statement the normal program statements are completed with an **Exit Sub** statement before the error handling routine begins. On completion of the error handling routine, the program is then terminated as normal with the **End Sub**

161

command. An example of the general syntax for using this in a VBA program is given below:

```
Sub progName()
On Error GoTo ErrorHandler
…
Exit Sub
ErrorHandler:
…
End Sub
```

To see how these statements could be used, consider the following examples.

This first takes the VBA macro that we developed in Chapter 3 which sets up the monthly changes. That is, it copies end of month sales to sales to date, then clears the Weekly sales ready for the next month's incoming sales, and finally increments the month number for the following month's data.

Listing 8.3

```
Sub updateSalesErrorhandling()
   On Error GoTo SheetMissingHandler
      Worksheets("Weeklysal").Select
      ActiveSheet.Unprotect
      Range("end_month_sales").Copy
      Range("sales_to_date").PasteSpecial xlValues
      Range("Week_Sales").ClearContents
      Range("Month_No") = Range("Month_No") + 1
      If (Range("Month_No").Value > 12) Then
         MsgBox "Please Start A New Annual Sheet"
      End If
      ActiveSheet.Protect
   Exit Sub
   SheetMissingHandler:    'error handling routine - sheet does not exist
    MsgBox prompt:="Entry Error- the weeklysal sheet does not exist"
End Sub
```

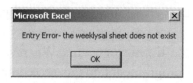

Figure 8.10 Error dialog box from Listing 8.3

The second example uses the **On Error Goto** statement to trap errors. The macro transfers to the *QuotientErrHandler* label if an attempt is made to divide by zero. On passing control to this section, the program will then display a **MsgBox** alerting the user to the fact that you cannot divide by zero. The code will input two integer variables called *first* and *second*. It will then divide *first* by *second* and output the result. However, if the user attempts to divide by zero, a run-time error will occur, which is the purpose of using the error trapping routine. The procedure is called *calQuotient* and is displayed in Listing 8.4.

Listing 8.4 Division by zero error trapping routine

```
Sub calQuotient()
    Worksheets("sheet3").Select
    On Error GoTo quotientErrHandler
    Dim first_number As Integer
    Dim second_number As Integer
    Dim quotient As Integer
    Dim Result As Range
        first_number = InputBox(prompt:="enter first number")
        second_number = InputBox(prompt:="enter second number")
        quotient = first_number / second_number
        Columns("B:B").ColumnWidth = 18
        Range("B1").Font.Bold = True
        Range("B1").Value = "Division Program"
        Range("B3:B5").Clear
        Range("B3").Value = "First Number ="
        Range("B4").Value = "Second Number ="
        Range("B5").Value = "Quotient  ="
        Range("C3:C5").Clear
        Range("C3").Value = first_number
        Range("C4").Value = second_number
        Set Result = Range("C5")
        Result.Value = quotient
        Result.Font.Bold = True
        Result.Borders(xlBottom).Weight = xlMedium
        Result.Borders(xlTop).Weight = xlMedium
        Exit Sub
        quotientErrHandler:
        MsgBox prompt:="Entry Error- you cannot divide by 0!"
            'division by zero error
End Sub
```

Figure 8.11 The run-time error message following an attempt to divide by 0

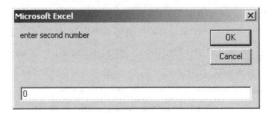

Figure 8.12 InputBox receiving second integer

This example procedure examines the *weeklysales* worksheet in the work-book SALESMAN.XLS and checks each of the cells using the UsedRange property to see if it contains a formula. If it does have a formula, then the contents of the cell will be emboldened, otherwise it will be left alone. The error trapping routine in this procedure is used to capture run-time errors, which in this procedure could only arise from the worksheet named *weeklySales* not existing. Thus, on entry to the error handling routine, see

---

Listing 8.5

```
Sub  boldFormulaCells()
    On Error GoTo errorHandler
    Dim cell As Range
    Worksheets("weeklysales").Select
    Activesheet.UnProtect
    For Each cell In ActiveSheet.UsedRange
        If cell.HasFormula Then
            cell.Font.bold = true
        End If
    Next
    Exit Sub

    errorHandler:
        MsgBox "Sheet does not Exist"
End Sub
```

Listing 8.5, a message box containing "Sheet does not exist" is displayed. Figure 8.13 displays the output screenshot when no error is encountered. Figure 8.14 displays the message on entry to the error handling routine.

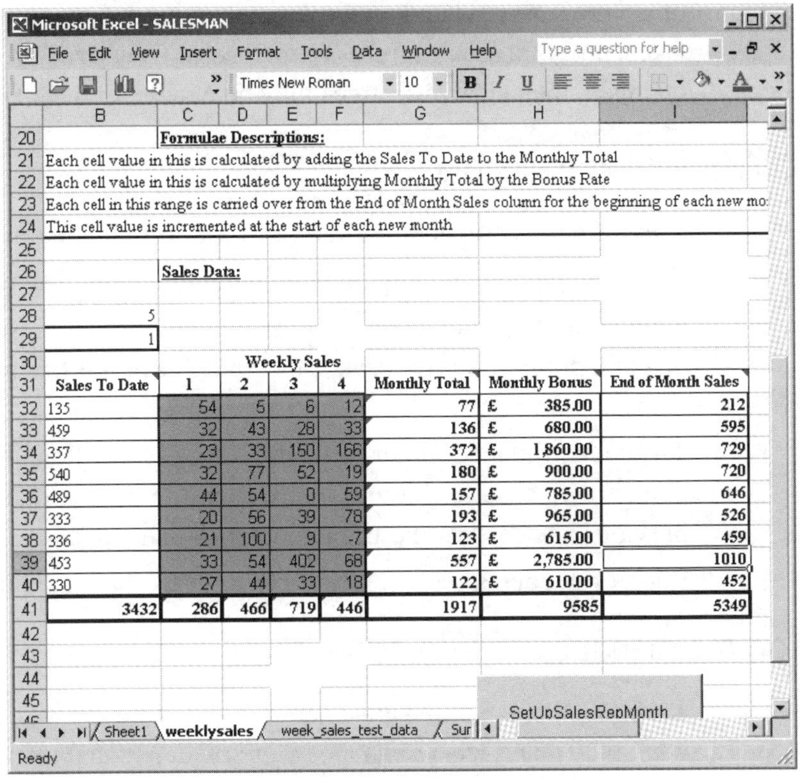

Figure 8.13 Listing 8.4 output when worksheet exists

Figure 8.14 MsgBox on entry to error handling routine

Maintenance of VBA programs

Maintenance can account for about 67 percent of time spent on a software development project. It is not just fixing program errors, but also making changes to adapt to user requirements. Maintenance may be necessary when other programs related to the system change. For example, if a VBA for Excel program uses an Access database, and the structure of the database has changed, then clearly changes may be needed to the VBA program as well.

Difficulties with maintenance

There are many difficulties that can arise from maintaining code as follows:

♦   It can sometimes be very difficult to maintain code that was written by another programmer. It might be difficult to discuss these problems with the original programmers, because they may have left the organisation, retired, or whatever.

♦   The code produced might be unstructured – or following no method as the person who produced it was a novice at the time! Code was produced in a previous standard of the implementation language.

♦   Poor, or no, documentation is likely to exacerbate maintenance difficulties.

Tips on maintenance of VBA code

♦   Take care when making any changes to existing software. Document clearly why, when and where changes were made, so that some sort of trace back can be made in the event of problems.

♦   Use the debugging facilities that were discussed earlier in this chapter to step through the code with the debugger, put in watches, breakpoints, and so on, so that you can ascertain what is happening. This can also help prevent crashes due to infinite loops, and so on.

♦   **Do not** eliminate program code unless you are sure that it isn't used! You might find that you may need it again at some later date. 'Comment out' lines of code that you think might be required rather than delete them. That way, you can always retrieve it in the future if required.

♦   Insert error checking where possible. Remember, the fallibility of human nature – if something can go wrong, it will!

Exercises

1 Explain briefly the distinction between syntax, compilation and logical errors.

2 Explain briefly why testing is necessary.

3 What debugging features of VBA would you use to check the value that a cell takes in a range, to see that each value is correct. Explain how you would do this?

4 Open a new workbook, call it ERROR.XLS and name two worksheets *mySheet1* and *mySheet2*. Create the following VBA macro, and run it.

```
Sub errors()
    Application.DisplayAlerts = True
    Worksheets("mySheet2").Delete
End Sub
```

Explain what has happened. Now change the line:

```
    Application.DisplayAlerts = True
```

so that it becomes

```
Application.DisplayAlerts = False
Worksheets("mySheet1").Delete
```

Now run the program again and explain what has changed.

5 Give reasons for using the Immediate window when using VBA?

6 Open the VBA Help system and read the sections on debugging.

7 Open the macro *getValidRepName* as shown below and run it to find a particular RepName. Test it by repeatedly typing in wrong RepNames before typing a correct one. Now create a range of test data and to ensure the program is working properly.

```
Sub getValidRepName()
    Dim thisRepName As Variant
    Dim myCell As Object
    Dim isFound As Boolean
    Worksheets("Weeklysales").Select
    isFound = False 'assume RepName repName is not found yet
    Do Until isFound
        thisRepName = InputBox(prompt:="enter a rep name")
        'for loop tries to find this representative name in list
        For Each myCell In Range("Rep_name")
            If myCell = thisRepName Then    'good – it has been found
```

```
                myCell.Interior.ColorIndex = 4
                isFound = True
                MsgBox "found at " & myCell.Address
            End If
        Next
    Loop
End Sub
```

8   Open the *getValidRepName* macro from the previous exercise. Click the cursor on the line **isFound** = **True**. Click on the breakpoint button. Now run the macro. The macro should stop (break) at line 7 and show you the debugger window. Make sure the Watch pane is visible. Select the variable *isFound* and click on the **Watch** button, then click **Add** to add it to the Watch pane. Inspect the value of *IsFound*. Also, in the same way, add watches to the variables, *myCell* and *thisRepName* and to the expression **myCell** = **thisRepName**. Look at their values in the Watch pane. Now start stepping through the macro – and keep an eye on the values in the Watch pane. This should help you get familiar with the debugger, and with the macro code.

9   Use the following macro to try out testing and debugging.

```
Sub setHighSales()
    Dim myCell As Object
    Worksheets("Weeklysales").Select
    ActiveSheet.Unprotect
    For Each myCell In Range("Week_sales")
        If myCell < 20 Then
            myCell.Interior.ColorIndex = 7
        ElseIf myCell > 20 And myCell < 40 Then
            myCell.Interior.ColorIndex = 8
        ElseIf myCell > 40 Then
            myCell.Interior.ColorIndex = 9
        End If
    Next
    ActiveSheet.Protect
End Sub
```

9 Subs and functions

Subroutines 170

Functions 172

Creating functions 174

Passing parameters 182

Exercises 186

Subroutines

Macros, also called *procedures*, or *subs*, can perform virtually any task. They can be used for clearing cells in an area of a worksheet, or sorting a list of items before printing it, and a multitude of other things. As programs become longer and more complex, so it becomes necessary to break them down into smaller parts where each part performs a specific task. There will usually be a main task which might then activate, or call, other tasks when necessary. This is known as modular programming and VBA facilitates this approach. For example, a complex sub can be made simpler by accessing or 'calling' another sub. The following example shows how this is done.

Calling subs

Suppose you needed to write code that enabled the user to select a range of cells, and then from the range chosen, output the number of valid cells (i.e. non-blank cells) using a message box. To implement this we will use two sub procedures. The first will be used to select the range, this will then 'call' the second sub procedure whose purpose will be to calculate the number of non-blank cells in the range. We have already seen a similar example in the previous chapter when we looked at the **Step over** tool for debugging.

To call a sub, you write its name followed by any arguments that are passed into it. In this example, we are not passing any arguments.

The two subs are *getRange* and *countValidCells* (Listings 9.1 and 9.2). The purpose of the *getRange* procedure is to enable the user to enter a cell range, and the procedure would select the cell range on the worksheet. It does this by using a range variable, *Rng*, stored from the InputBox method of the Application object. The **If Rng Is Nothing Then** statement checks to see that the user has selected a range. If not, then an "Operation Cancelled" message appears, otherwise the selected range is highlighted. The next statement will call the *CountValidCells* sub. This works by creating two variables: an integer variable to store the number of non-blank cells, and a string variable called *strCount* to store a string version of this variable so that it can be formatted for use with a **MsgBox** function. The statement: **myCount = Application.CountA(Selection)** uses the CountA method for counting all non-blank cells in the range, and the statement: **strCount = Str(myCount)** converts the integer variable to a string variable for use in the **MsgBox**.

Listing 9.1 The GetRange sub

```
'Highlights selected range and then calls a sub called CountValidRange
'which will count non-empty cells in selected range
Sub getRange()
    Dim Rng As Range
    Set Rng = Application.InputBox(prompt:="Enter range", Type:=8)
    If Rng Is Nothing Then
        MsgBox "Operation Cancelled"
    Else
        Rng.Select
    End If
        CountValidCells
End Sub
```

Listing 9.2 The CountValidCells sub

```
Sub countValidCells()
    Dim myCount As Integer
    Dim strCount As String
    myCount = Application.CountA(Selection)
    strCount = Str(myCount)
    answerString = "There are " + strCount + " valid cell(s)in this selection"
    MsgBox answerString, vbInformation, "Count Cells"
End Sub
```

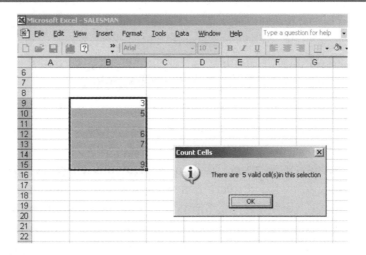

Figure 9.1 Output of Listings 9.1 and 9.2

171

Functions

Any Excel user will be aware of functions such as Sum, Average, Count, and so on. These functions can be used from Excel, just like defining a formula in a cell, i.e., begin with the '=' sign, then select the function required from the Function list box. These are the built-in functions. The idea behind a function is that you send data into it and the function sends back, or returns, an answer. These examples show how built-in functions are used in Excel:

```
=Tan (0.7)
```

The trigonometric **Tan** function returns the value of Tan(0.7) = 0.842288

```
=Count(C1:C4)
```

The **Count** function returns the number of cells in the range C1:C4 = 4.

```
varAnswer = Application.WorksheetFunction.Sum(Range("E1:E32"))
```

This statement will call **WorksheetFunction.Sum** to sum the range from E1 to E32 and assign the result to *varAnswer*. In this function, you send in to it the cell range, and return the sum of that range.

```
varAnswer = Application.WorksheetFunction.Sum(Range("A1",
Range("A1").End(xlDown)))
```

This statement will use **WorksheetFunction.Sum** to sum the range from E1 to the last active cell in the column and assign the result to *varAnswer*.

```
If LCase(Selection.value)= "" then MsgBox "Good"
```

This statement uses the **LCase** function within the test and translates the string into lower case letters. This is a very useful function when there is a possibility of the user selecting a non-tested text case. You send it a text string and it returns the same string in lower-case.

In all of the above examples we can see that one or more values, or *arguments*, are send into the function and a value, the answer, is returned. These built-in functions can be used with the VBA language and we have already used some of them in previous chapters. We have come across functions that convert data from one type to another – such as **Val (string)** for converting string format to numeric, or **Str (number)** for converting a numeric into a string representation (see Chapter 5). We have also used functions to manipulate strings. The following example uses more string conversion functions.

The example in Listing 9.3 allows the user to select a number of cells then checks each of them to see if there is a formula. If there is, a message box is displayed giving the address of the cell and its formula. If not, no message box will be displayed. The test to find out if each cell uses a formula is the line that reads:

If Mid(Cell.Formula, 1, 1) = "=" Then

This line uses the built-in string function **Mid()**. This takes three arguments: the first looks at the cell formula, the second refers to the position in the string (in this case 1) and the third refers to the number of characters to be extracted (in this case 1). Clearly, if this value is the '=' character, then there must be a formula in the cell, since every cell containing a formula begins with '='.

Listing 9.3 Example of using the built-in String function Mid()

```
Sub addressFormulasMsgBox()  'Displays the address and formula
    For Each Cell In Selection
        If Mid(Cell.Formula, 1, 1) = "=" Then
            MsgBox "The formula in " & Cell.Address(rowAbsolute:=False, _
                columnAbsolute:=False) & " is:  " & Cell.Formula, vbInformation
        End If
    Next
End Sub
```

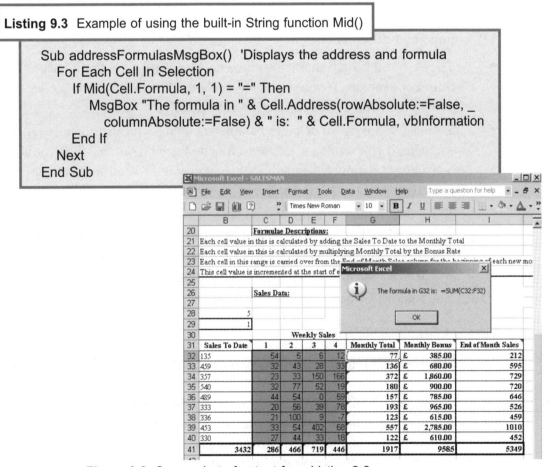

Figure 9.2 Screenshot of output from Listing 9.3

Creating functions

The last example shows how you can use VBA built-in functions in your procedures. You can also create your own custom functions in VBA. Creating a function is not quite the same thing as a sub, for a function always has a specific objective – to return a value! This is the key difference between a function and an ordinary procedure. In general, you should use functions rather than subs to create custom procedures.

A value returned by a function could be anything from a string to a numeric value, such as an integer, or even a Boolean *true* or *false* to inform the calling statement that the function has succeeded or failed.

Defining a function

A function is defined in a similar way to a procedure, but with a few important differences:

- The keyword **Function** is substituted for **Sub**. **End Function** replaces **End Sub**. For example, if you wanted to declare a function named *thisOne* then you would need to write **Function thisOne()**.

- You can specify zero or more parameters along with their data types. For example, if you wanted to declare a function named *thisOne* that would use one integer parameter called *x*, then you would need a statement like: **Function thisOne (x As Integer)**.

- The function must return a certain type of value. This is specified after the argument list. For example, if you wanted to declare the function *thisOne* that would use one integer parameter *x*, and return a Currency value, you would write the declaration **Function thisOne(x As Integer)As Currency**.

- You return a value by assigning it to the name of the function.

Parameters and arguments

The terms *parameter* and *argument* are not synonymous. A *parameter* is the term that is used to describe the form of data items associated with a function declaration. For example, in **Function doubleValue (anyNumber As Integer)**, *anyNumber* is a parameter, because it tells the function what form the data that is being passed into it will take: in this case integer. The value used in place of the parameter when we make the function call is called an *argument*. In this example, i.e., *doubleValue (12)* then the argument is the integer 12. One can think of a parameter as a variable and an argument the value that the variable takes in a specific situation.

This simple example function is called *doubleValue* – for its purpose is to double any integer value. Before writing the code, note the following:

- There will be one parameter associated with this function, and that parameter – called *AnyNumber* – will be of integer data type. Within the function, *AnyNumber* is used as if it where a normal variable.

- The type of the value to be returned will be an integer. Notice how the data type to be returned is given after the argument declaration in parentheses.

- The function is being named *doubleValue*, and the function will take the value of the argument being passed to it, and multiply it by two.

```
Function  doubleValue(AnyNumber As Integer) As Integer
    doubleValue =  AnyNumber * 2
End Function
```

Calling a function

A function can be called as a direct call in Excel, i.e. you use it like any other built-in function, by clicking on the cell where it is to be used and typing '=' then writing its name – in this case – *doubleValue* followed by the value that you want doubled. (Remember, it has to be an Integer). Figure 9.3 shows how the above function could be called using the value of the argument =12.

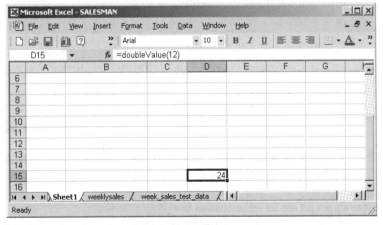

Figure 9.3 Calling the function doubleValue() in Excel

This is very similar to the way in which any other Excel function is called, i.e. the function is executed by beginning with the =sign in the active cell.

The function *doubleValue()* can be called within other sub or function procedures. For example, in the following macro called *testDouble()*, a call to the function *doubleValue* is made with the line: **MsgBox "the value is: " & doubleValue(37)**

```
Sub testDouble()
    MsgBox "the value is: " & doubleValue(37)
End Sub
```

The function *doubleValue()* can also be used within a cell formula, e.g.

```
=doubleValue(F10)
```

Take note

Both the argument passed to the function doubleValue() and the return value was declared as being Integer. If you therefore pass a non-integer value, the result will not be as expected. For example, "=doubleValue(3.4)" will return 6 (the truncated value).

This example rewrites the calling subs example from pages 170–171, by implementing the called procedure as a function instead of a sub. The procedures are written in Listings 9.4 and 9.5. To translate the called procedure to a function you will see the following changes have been made:

- The called procedure *countValidCells* begins with the word **Function**, and an **End Function** statement is used to terminate it (see Listing 9.5).

- A range parameter has been passed into the function, and we have designed the function such that a string is returned that will contain the number of cells in the valid range (see Listing 9.5).

- The function value is returned *in the function* by the statement: **countValidCells = Str(myCount)**

- The function value is returned *to the calling procedure* by the statement: **thisCount = countValidCells(Rng)**

- The function value is output in the calling sub procedure using the message box statement:

```
MsgBox answerString, vbInformation, "Count Cells"
```

Listing 9.4 Sub GetRange

```
Sub getRange()
    Dim thisCount As String
    Dim Rng As Range
    Set Rng = Application.InputBox(prompt:="Enter range", Type:=8)
    If Rng Is Nothing Then
        MsgBox "Operation Cancelled"
    Else
        Rng.Select
    End If
    thisCount = countValidCells(Rng)
    answerString = "There are "+ thisCount + " valid cell(s)in this selection"
    MsgBox answerString, vbInformation, "Count Cells"
End Sub
```

Listing 9.5 Function CountValidCells

```
Function countValidCells(Rng As Range) As String
    Dim myCount  As Integer
    Dim strCount As String
    myCount = Application.CountA(Selection)
    strCount = Str(myCount)
    countValidCells = Str(myCount)
End Function
```

Worked example

This example function is intended to work with the *weeklysales* worksheet of the SALESMAN.XLS workbook. Its purpose is to find the highest weekly sales in the *week_sales* named range. We have used a function for this purpose because we require a value to be returned: i.e., the highest value. The function has been named *getMaxSales*, and searches through all the cells in the *week_sales* range to find the largest value, which will be an integer. The function therefore, will return an integer value. No arguments are passed into this function. The function definition is shown in Listing 9.6, and the screenshot in Figure 9.4 displays the result of 402 when the function is executed by calling it in cell G28.

Listing 9.6 Function getMaxSales()

```
Function getMaxSales() As Integer
    Dim maxSales As Integer
    Dim Cell As Object
    maxSales = 0 'assume the lowest possible
    For Each Cell In Range("Week_sales")
        If Cell > maxSales Then
            maxSales = Cell 'we've found a bigger sales
        End If
    Next
    getMaxSales = maxSales
End Function
```

In the function definition, there are no arguments associated with it – the parentheses for the name are empty. However, the return type is an integer (i.e. a maximum value of sales).

The function works by declaring a variable called *maxSales* that is used to contain the largest number in the range *week_sales*. The initial value assigned to *maxSales* is 0, which is the smallest value that the actual maximum can be, and therefore has to be used initially for comparison with all cell values in the range *week_sales*. Each cell in the **For** loop is examined to see if its current value is > *maxSales*. This comparison is implemented using the statement **If Cell > maxSales Then maxSales = Cell**. This means that if a cell value is greater than the current value of *maxSales* then assign the contents of *maxSales* to *Cell*, otherwise leave the *maxSales* value unchanged. When the loop is completed, the contents of the variable *maxSales* will contain the maximum sales value in the range. Notice that after the loop is completed, then *maxSales* is assigned to the return value, i.e., the function named *getMaxSales*. We can see this function running using the worksheet *weeklysales*.

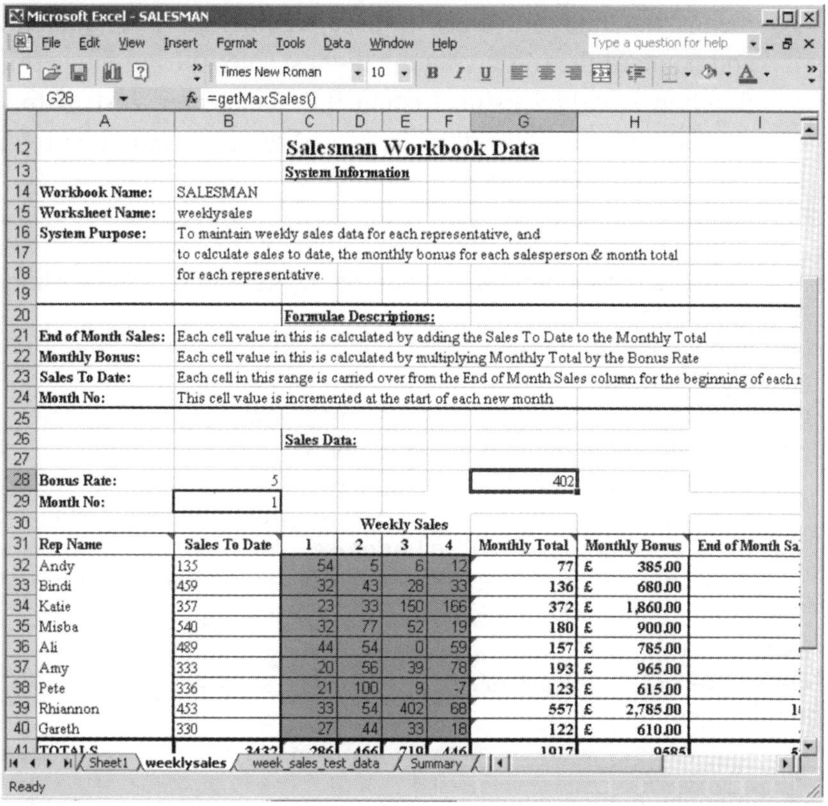

Figure 9.4 Screenshot of Function getMaxSales() Called at cell G28

Using parameters to extend the scope of functions

Parameters provide a way of transferring data between sub procedures and function procedures. We can often extend the capabilities of a function by using parameters. For example, suppose we wanted to extend the *getMaxSales* function that was developed in Listing 9.6 to provide the cell address and the RepName of the salesperson who recorded the maximum sale. The extended function procedure, called *GetMaxSalesInfo*, is shown in Listing 9.7. Notice that in the new function definition, we have passed two arguments: one called *maxSalesAddress*, and the other called *thisRepName*. The function only differs from that of Listing 9.6 in that whenever *maxSales > myCell*, *maxSalesAddress* is assigned to *myCell.Addess* and *thisRepName* is assigned to *Worksheets("weeklysales").Cells(myCell.Row, 1).Value*. This means that the final values of these arguments will contain the cell address, and name of the rep giving the highest sales during the period. Notice, this function is called using Listing 9.8. This uses a **MsgBox** to output the maximum sales, the cell address, and the corresponding rep name.

Listing 9.7 Function getMaxSales()

```
Function GetMaxSalesInfo(maxSalesAddress As String, thisRepName As
    String) As Integer
    Dim maxSales As Integer
    Dim myCell As Object
    maxSales = 0                    'initialise to the lowest possible value
    For Each myCell In Range("Week_sales")
        If myCell > maxSales Then
            maxSales = myCell          'we have found a bigger sales
            maxSalesAddress = myCell.Address
            thisRepName = Worksheets("Weeklysales").Cells(myCell.Row,1).Value
        End If
    Next
    GetMaxSalesInfo = maxSales
End Function
```

Listing 9.8 Calling the extended function

```
Sub testMaxSalesInfo()
    Dim theAddress As String
    Dim theRepName As String
    Dim theMax As Integer
    theMax = GetMaxSalesInfo(theAddress, theRepName)
    MsgBox "the maximum is: " & theMax & vbCrLf & _
        "the address is: " & theAddress & vbCrLf & _
        "the rep name is: " & theRepName
End Sub
```

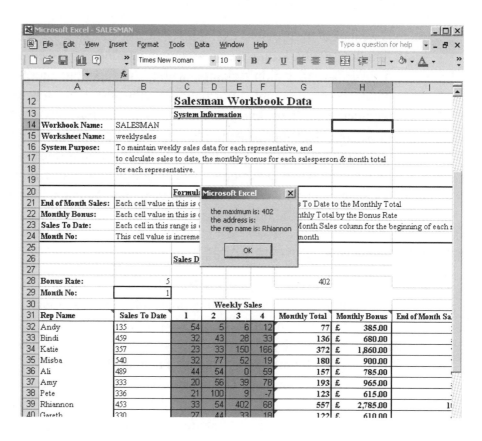

Figure 9. 5 Screenshot of Listing 9.8

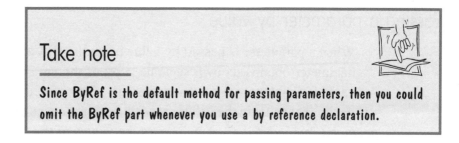

Take note

Since ByRef is the default method for passing parameters, then you could
omit the ByRef part whenever you use a by reference declaration.

Passing parameters

If we look at the previous examples of the use of functions, we see that in the function *doubleValue* there was one parameter passed into it, called *anyNumber*, that didn't change within the function: the purpose of this parameter was to supply information. On the other hand, when we passed the parameters *theRepName* and *theAddess* to the function *GetMaxSalesInfo* these could be changed within it, for their purpose was to represent the rep name and cell address associated with the maximum sales value. Since the maximum sales is a variable, then so are the values of *theRepName* and *theAddress* and therefore their values could change within the function. There are two methods of passing arguments: by *reference* and by *value*.

Passing a parameter by references

When a parameter is passed by reference, a reference to the original argument is passed to the calling procedure. The result is that if a change is made to the parameter in the passed procedure, then that changed value is passed back to the called procedure. In VBA, the default method of passing arguments is by reference. That is, if neither **ByRef** nor **ByVal** is specified then **ByRef** is assumed. The syntax for declaring a **ByRef** parameter is to insert the keyword **ByRef** before the parameter list is declared in the parentheses following the function name. For example, suppose we had a function called *thisFunct* that used a string parameter called *myStr*, and we wanted to pass this parameter by reference, then the declaration would be:

```
Function thisFunct (ByRef myStr as String)
```

Passing a parameter by value

When a parameter is passed by value using the **ByVal** keyword, the called parameter obtains its own separate copy of the variable. The value of the variable can therefore be changed in the called procedure without affecting its original value in the calling procedure. This means that as in the function *GetMaxSalesInfo*, when it changes the values of the parameters on lines 8 and 9, these changes also take place in the calling procedure. So in line 5 of *TestMaxSalesInfo*, the two actual parameters *theAddress* and *theRepname* are also changed, when the function is called. The syntax for declaring a ByVal parameter is to insert the keyword **ByVal** before the parameter list is declared in the parentheses following the function name. If we had a function called *thisFunct* that used a string parameter called *myStr*, and we wanted to pass this parameter by value, then the function declaration would be:

```
Function thisFunct (ByVal myStr as String)
```

Worked example

To see how passing parameters by value and by reference work in practice, let's look at an example of what happens when we pass parameters by reference and by value.

Consider the function, *sqNum*, which squares an integer, and then the sub, *testSqNum*, which makes a call to *sqNum*. Listing 9.9 displays the sub *testSqNum* code. Notice that an Integer variable called *passVal* is declared and assigned the value 10 in the sub. The call to the pass by value function is sandwiched between the two message box displays: the first displays *passVal* before it is passed to the function, the second displays *passVal* after being passed to the function. Notice from Figure 9.6 that the value of *passVal* passed back to the sub after the function call is 10. That's because it has been passed by value and that means that it cannot change when passed to the function.

Now consider what happens when the parameter is passed by reference as shown in Listing 9.10. When the code is run, the *passVal* passed back to the sub after the function is called has the value 20 (see Figure 9.7). This is because it has been passed by reference and that means that it can be changed when passed to the function.

Listing 9.9

```
Sub testSqNum ()
    Dim passVal As Integer
    PassVal = 10
    MsgBox "Number passed into square function is = " & passVal
    MsgBox "Function value is = " & sqNum (passVal) & vbCrLf & _
    "Number passed back to square function is = " & passVal
End Sub
```

Listing 9.10 Passing a parameter by reference

```
Function sqNum (ByRef passVal As Integer)
   SqNum = passVal * passVal
   PassVal = 20
End Function
```

Now let us see what happens when we pass the parameter by value instead. You can see from Figure 9.6 that the first message box shows the number going into the function is 10, as expected, but the second message box shows that the value passed back to the calling procedure is also 10 not 20. This is because the parameter has been passed by value – giving a result as expected.

Listing 9.11 Passing a parameter by value

```
Function sqNum (ByVal passVal As Integer)
   SqNum = passVal * passVal
   PassVal = 20
End Function
```

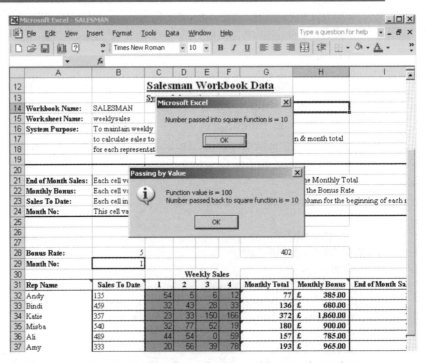

Figure 9.6 Screenshot with MsgBox displays with pass by value

184

Figure 9.7 Screenshot of the second MsgBox display after value passed by reference

Comparison of ByRef and ByVal

When passing parameters to procedures ByRef is faster than ByVal because passing by reference gives instant access to the parameter's value. However, the VBA programmer has to decide whether passing a parameter by reference is likely to have any harmful side effects on the parameter in the calling procedure. If this possibility exists then passing by value will be the sensible choice.

Exercises

1   Open a new workbook using a new module, write the VBA code in Listings 9.4 and 9.5. Run the subprogram to make sure it works correctly.

2   Write a function called *TrebleMe* that takes a integer value and multiplies it by 3. Test this function procedure by using a blank worksheet and enter =TrebleMe (30) in cell B3.

3   Write a function called *AddTwo* that will take two integer parameters and return their sum.

4   Write a function called *AddTwo* that will take two parameters as string values and return their sum as a string value.

5   Open the *weeklysales* sheet of the SALESMAN workbook. Create a function called *IsValidRepName* that will take a repName as a parameter and returns True if the repName exists in the range on the worksheet. Test your function using **=IsRepName (Jack)**, and **=IsRepName (Rhiannon)** using any blank cells on the worksheet.

Write the following sub procedure for testing the function.

```
Sub TestIsValidRepName ()
    Dim tryRep As String
    TryRep = InputBox "enter a repName for testing"
    MsgBox "the repName is valid: " & IsValidRepName (tryRep)
End Sub
```

Amend your function from (3) so that it has an extra parameter to pass back the address of the cell in which that repName is found. Test your function.

Amend your function from (4) so that it has a third extra parameter to pass back the value of the miles to date for that RepName. Test your function.

Try out the pass **ByRef** and **ByVal** example in 5.4 and 5.5.

6   Study the following sub procedure and try to find out what it does.

```
Sub IsActiveCellEmpty()
    Dim stFunctionName As String, stCellReference As String
    stFunctionName = "isblank"
    StCellReference = ActiveCell.Address
    MsgBox Evaluate (stFunctionName & "(" & stCellReference & ")")
End Sub
```

10 Using forms

User forms 188

The form design 194

Event procedures 199

Creating event procedure code . . 200

Creating context sensitive Help . . 203

Designing for the end user 209

Exercises 212

User forms

When we create or use Windows applications, our primary means of input is through dialog boxes. We have seen these several times previously. In this chapter, you will learn to create our own custom dialog boxes. To do this however, you need to start with something to design on, in the same way as a painter needs a canvas to begin painting. This canvas in VBA is called a *user form*.

Designing user forms

To build an application that uses forms, you must first design the form. Enter the VBE from Excel using **[Alt]+[F11]**. Make sure that both the Project Explorer and Properties panes are visible (see Figure 10.1). If they are not, use **View > Project Explorer** or **View > Properties**. To add a form, use **Insert > UserForm**. A blank form will appear. A great deal of thought is needed now as this will be the user's interface to the application.

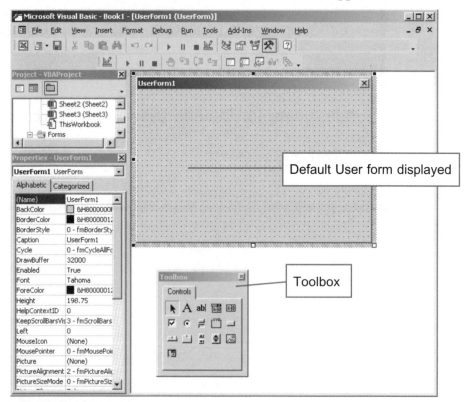

Figure 10.1 The screen layout when a new user form is selected

The Properties pane

The Project Explorer has already been described in Chapter 3. The Properties pane will contain a description of the object currently selected. In Figure 10.1, it is displaying for *UserForm1* those properties that can be changed at design time. These include things like the background colour (**BackColor**), border colour (**BorderColor**), border style (**BorderStyle**), font, and many more. Notice that the properties all have default values – the ones that will apply if no changes are made to them during design time. Notice the properties **Name** and **Caption**. These are not the same thing, even though it may have the same value (see Figure 10.1). The **Name** is used by VBA programs to access the object, whereas the **Caption** refers to the text displayed on the Title bar.

The Toolbox

The Toolbox contains a number of controls that you can use during design time. These are similar to the Control toolbox on the **View** menu. When you select a control from the toolbox, you can position and resize it as with all Windows programs by using the mouse. The available controls are:

for pointing and selecting controls

Label – generally used for prompting Textbox input.

TextBox – for collecting user input, e.g. a person's name or address.

ComboBox – lets you select an item from a list or type an item which is not on the list.

ListBox – lets the user select one or more items from a list.

CheckBox – can be checked or unchecked to turn options on or off.

OptionButton or **RadioButton** – lets the user select one and only one item from a list.

ToggleButton – shows the user whether an item is selected.

Frame – used to group together a set of related controls.

CommandButton – when clicked will trigger some event.

TabStrip – lets you view different sets of information for related controls.

MultiPage – presents multiple screens of information as a single set.

ScrollBar – lets the user set numeric values.

SpinButton – can be used to scroll through a range of values or a list of items, or to change the value displayed in a text box.

Image – used for adding an Image to a form.

Adding controls to a user form

To add a control to a user form, point and click on the control in the Toolbox then drag to the point on the form where it is required and click.

In this example, we will develop a Form that inputs two numbers and provides three buttons on the form: one to add them, one to multiply them and one to quit. The steps are:

1   Open a new workbook and press **[Alt]+[F11]** to go to the VBE. Select **Insert > UserForm**. A blank user form and the toolbox palette will be displayed.

2   Change the **Caption** on the user form from *UserForm1* to *Calculator* by clicking the Caption property (see Figure 10.2) in the Properties pane.

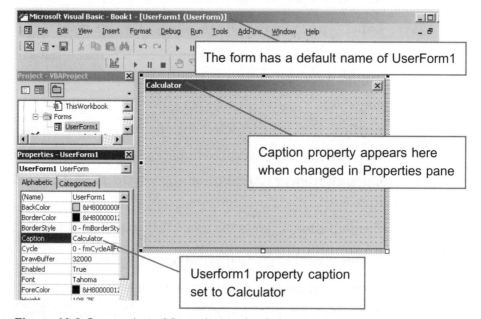

Figure 10.2 Screenshot of form design for Calculator

3 We now need to create some labels and text boxes to allow the data to be input. First, click the **Label** tool and drop the label on to the position shown on the form. Resize it using the mouse. Rename it *Number One*. Do the same for the other labels. Create the text boxes as shown in Figure10.3. Click the **Text** tool and drop to the position on the form as shown. Now set the Name property from the default values of *TextBox1* and *TextBox2* to *firstbox* and *secondbox* respectively.

4 Create three buttons and label them 'ADD', 'MULTIPLY' and 'QUIT' by setting the Caption properties. Set their Names to *add*, *multiply* and *quit*.

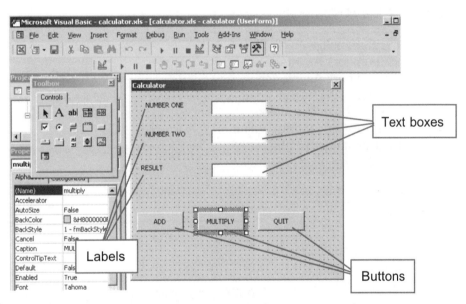

Figure 10.3 Screenshot displaying the labels, text boxes and buttons

5 Now it's time to start writing the event handler code. First, double-click the ADD button. You should see the lines **Private: Sub add_Click()** and **End Sub** from where you can enter the code. Enter the code as shown in Listing 10.1. This is the event handler's VBA code for the ADD button. Repeat the process, entering Listing 10.2 for the MULTIPLY button and Listing 10.3 for the QUIT button.

6 Test the program by clicking the **Run** button on the Standard toolbar and trying different combinations of numbers in the boxes and clicking on the various buttons.

> **Listing 10.2** The Multiply event handler

```
Private Sub multiply_Click()
   Dim number1 As Integer
   Dim number2 As Integer
   Dim result As Integer
   number1 = firstBox.Value
   number2 = secondBox.Value
   result = number1 * number2
   resultBox.Value = result
End Sub
```

> **Listing 10.3** The Quit event handler

```
Private Sub quit_Click ()
   Unload calculator
End Sub
```

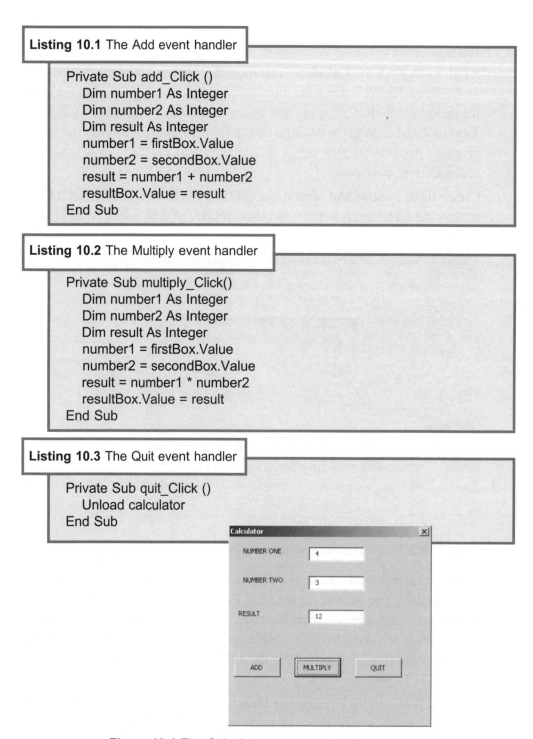

Figure 10.4 The Calculator program at work

Data entry forms

This example has a custom dialog box in the SALESMAN workbook to enable the user to input a new rep name along with the corresponding sales to date. This data would then be transferred to the *Weeklysales* sheet and appended to the repName list, along with the corresponding sales.

The purpose of the form is to insert an extra row and add the representative name in the *repName* list. When the data is transferred to the worksheet not only does the new details have to be appended, but the totals figure in the 'Sales To Date' column will have to be increased to include the sales for the new rep. This means that if a new rep is inserted – Keith in the example – then the sales for Keith, shown as 525, will be added to the previous total for sales to date giving a new value of 4846 (see Figure 10.6). The implementation of this VBA program is discussed later, after dealing with the form design.

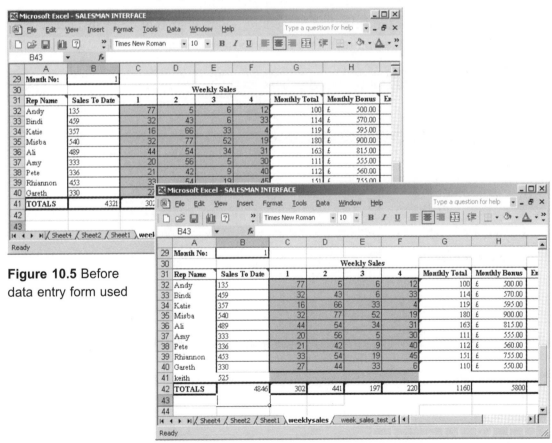

Figure 10.5 Before data entry form used

Figure 10.6 The Rep Names list appended to include a new RepName and Sales to Date

The form design

We need to create a form to provide the user with a means of entering the rep name and the rep sales to date. The form design is shown in Figure 10.7. The form Caption property has been called 'Add a Rep'. Two text boxes have been created: one for the new rep name, the other for the sales. Labels for the two buttons and other controls are also included. A Frameset has been added to surround the related items: rep name and sales, and its caption is 'Enter Details'. There is also a list box, which is used to display the existing rep names. There are two buttons: one to add details to the worksheet, and one to cancel the action.

Three event handlers are required to implement this task:

* One for the **AddDetails** button on the form;

* One for the **Cancel** button on the form;

* One for the **Initialize** procedure. There is no button for this because its called automatically when the form is first opened.

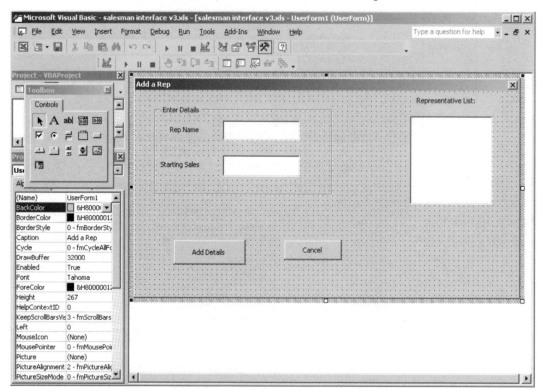

Figure 10.7 Design of the Add Rep form to SALESMAN Workbook.

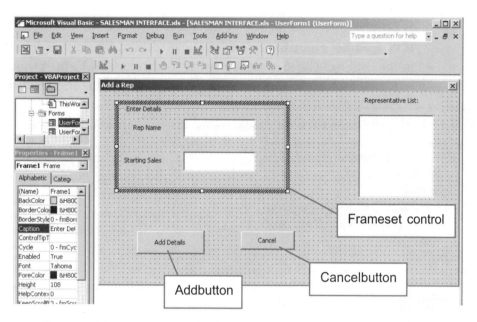

Figure 10.8 Screenshot Illustrating the Setting of Object Properties

The following Names have been assigned to the form components by setting their values in the Properties window:

RepBox: the text box used to store the rep name;

SalesBox: the text box used to store the sales name;

RepList: the list box used to store the rep list names.

The event handlers

The purpose of this code is to enable the user to enter a new rep name using the textbox (the name for this variable has been set in the Properties and is called *RepBox*), along with the corresponding sales for the Rep through the Starting Sales textbox. There is also a listbox included so that the user can check to see that they do not duplicate the entry of a rep name.

The Initialize() procedure

When the user runs a form the *User_Form_Initialize()* procedure is always invoked first because its purpose is to initialize any variables. In this case, we see that (Listing 10.4) *RepBox* is assigned an empty value, and *SalesBox*

195

is assigned the value 0. The next statement uses a **For Each cell in Range ("rep_name")** loop to take each name in the range and to display all the reps in the list box. The statement **Replist.AddItem.Cell.Value** inside the loop will take each cell value in the range and add it to the *RepList* listbox.

```
Private Sub UserForm_Initialize()
    RepBox = ""
    SalesBox = "0"
    For Each Cell In Range ("rep_name")
       RepList.AddItem Cell.Value
    Next
End Sub
```

The AddButton_Click() event

The event handler (Listing 10.5) works by checking to see if the value in the textbox called *RepBox* is empty. If it is, then the message "Enter a name for the rep to be added" is delivered, followed by setting the focus to the *RepBox* object by using the **statement .SetFocus**. This will ensure that the focus will continue to be on the *RepBox* object, forcing the user to enter a value for this. When a non-empty value is input the focus then switches to getting a value from the user for the starting sales. The initial value of this variable is 0.

The next group of statements uses **With Worksheets ("weeklysales").Range ("total")** to access properties and methods of the object called *total*. If you study the worksheets in Figures 10.5 and 10.6, you will see that it is at cell address A42. **newSumSales = salesBox.Value + .Offset (0, 1)** will assign the *newSumSales* variable to the current value of the *SalesBox*, plus the *.offset (0, 1)* value. Look at the worksheet in Figure 10.5 and you will see that this offset contains the current total. The new total will be stored in *newSumSales*. An entire row is then inserted relative to the total object using **.EntireRow.Insert**.

Next, the data is entered using the next two statements, i.e. **Offset (-1, 0) = RepBox.Value**. Note: we use *Offset (-1, 0)* because the new rep name needs to be immediately above the total object. Similarly the position of the

Listing 10.5 The AddButton event handler

```
Private Sub AddButton_Click ()
  RepBox.SetFocus
  With RepBox
    If .Value = "" Then
      MsgBox "Enter a name for the rep to be added"
      .SetFocus
    End If
    If .Value = "" Then
      MsgBox "Enter a sales value for the rep given"
      salesBox.SetFocus
    End If
  End With
  With Worksheets ("weeklysales").Range ("total")
    newSumSales = salesBox.Value + .Offset(0, 1)
    .EntireRow.Insert
    .Offset(-1, 0) = RepBox.Value
    .Offset(-1, 1) = salesBox.Value
    .Offset(0, 1) = newSumSales
    Range ("sales_to_date", .Offset (-1, 1)).Name = "sales_to_date"
  End With
  Replist.AddItem  RepBox.Value
  Unload Me
End Sub
```

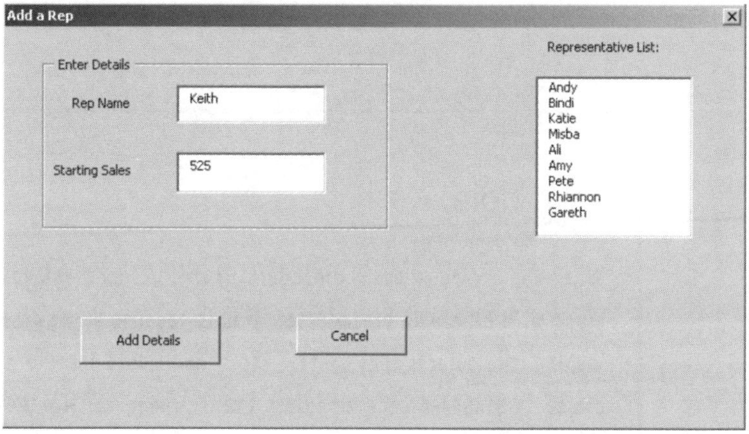

Figure10.9 Screenshot of form during the program run

corresponding new rep sales to date would have to be at one column to the right of this reference, i.e. *Offset (-1, 1)*. Next, the value of the *newSumSales* needs to be inserted in the cell to the right of the position of the total object, i.e. *Offset (0, 1)* and finally, we need to set the new *sales_to_date* range name to the old range plus the cell created with the new sales to date entry, since this is going to be the appended sales to date range, ready for any further additions. This is accomplished by using the statement: **Range ("sales_to_date", .Offset (-1, 1)).Name = "sales_to_date"**.

The **With** block ends in the usual way with **End With**. Next, the **RepList.AddItem.Cell.Value** will append the list with the extra name on the form before **Unload Me** will unload the form.

The CancelButton_Click()Event

The code for this event is very simple and requires only the statements **Unload Me** and **End** (Listing 10.6).

Listing 10.6 The Cancel event code

```
Private Sub CancelButton_Click ()
    Unload Me
    End
End Sub
```

Take note

When you create an event procedure, it will not be displayed in the macro list along with other sub procedures. This is because event procedures are stored 'behind' the objects that contain them, and would therefore not be written or stored in standard code modules. Event procedures are *private* in that their code is not visible in the standard modules as sub procedures are. This is why event procedure code begins with the keyword **Private** before the word **Sub**.

Event procedures

We have seen examples of events in this chapter. For example, the Click event that is activated when a Command button is clicked. Other events occur in Excel, for example, when a workbook is opened, or when a new worksheet is created, or when a chart is printed. The VBA programmer can write code that activates whenever an Excel event of the type just described occur. This code is placed in an event procedure. There are many event procedures that can be used – too many for coverage in this book, and therefore we will look only at a couple of examples here. Appendix 2 shows a list of event procedures for each object. There are, excluding control events discussed earlier, four objects in Excel that can contain events. They are:

* Worksheet
* Chart
* Workbook
* Application.

Not all events are defined by all objects. In general, however, if an object has an event, its parent object will also have the same event. For example, the Change event is contained at the lowest level by the worksheet object, and its parent (the workbook object) also has this event, called *Workbook_SheetSelectionChange*. In turn, the workbook object's parent, the application, also has a Change event. (Application-level events work slightly differently than other events.)

Note also that Chart events only apply to Chart sheets, and not to Chart objects embedded in sheets.

Take note

The *only* code that should be in these modules are event procedures or declarations for these modules. Do not put your own macros or functions in these modules as they will not be visible or usable other than inthe named event procedures.

Creating event procedure code

You cannot write event procedure code using a standard code module, because the code resides behind the objects that contain them. To create an event procedure you will need to follow the steps shown below:

1   From the VBE, choose: **View** > **Project Explorer**.

2   In the Project Explorer, you will see a list of all the open workbooks (Figure 10.10). Locate your workbook in the list, and expand that branch. You'll see a folder called *Microsoft Excel Objects*. Expand this branch.

3   There will be an icon for each worksheet and chart sheets – if any – in your workbook, and an entry called *thisWorkbook*. To add a *thisWorkbook* event procedure, or a Worksheet level event procedure, right-click on the icon and choose **View Code** from the menu.

4   At the top of the module code window, there are two drop-down boxes. In the one on the left, select *Workbook* and in the one on the right, select the name of the event you want to add. In this example, I have selected the *Workbook_Open* event procedure. Excel will automatically insert the event code shell: the **Sub Workbook_Open()** and **End Sub** statements.

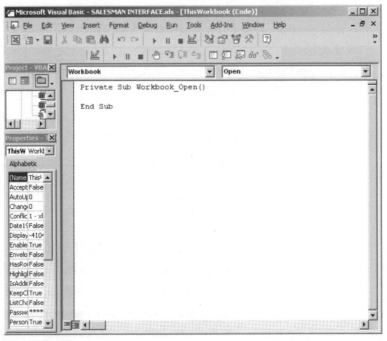

Figure 10.10 Creating an event procedure

The following event procedure (Listing 10.7) prevents the user from closing the active workbook until the value in A1of *Sheet1* is non-empty. Notice the event is called *Workbook_BeforeClose* and the code shell would be inserted by the steps described earlier. The code works by checking to see if the value in cell A1 is empty using the statement: **If Worksheets ("Sheet1").Range ("A1").Value = "" Then**. If true, then the Cancel parameter is set to True, cancelling the operation. A message box is also displayed informing the user why the workbook has not closed (see Figure10.11).

Listing 10.7 Event procedure code for Workbook_BeforeClose

```
Private Sub Workbook_BeforeClose (Cancel As Boolean)
    If Worksheets ("Sheet1").Range ("A1").Value = "" Then
        Cancel = True
        MsgBox "You cannot close until A1 is not empty"
    End If
End Sub
```

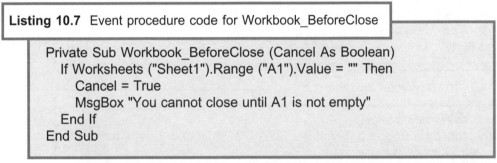

Figure 10.11 Illustration of Event Procedure Workbook_BeforeClose ()

This example is a variation of the *Auto_Open* sub procedure that was developed in Listing 3.3. A *Workbook_Open* event procedure is written that will call the *dayWeekMessage ()* sub as shown in Listing 10.9. This sub has essentially been described in Chapter 3. The *Workbook_Open* event procedure therefore is as shown in Listing 10.8. Notice the only code here is the call to the sub *dayWeekMessage*.

Listing 10.8 The Workbook_Open event procedure

```
Private Sub Workbook_Open ()
    dayWeekMessage
End Sub
```

Listing 10.9 The dayWeekMessage sub

```
Sub dayWeekMessage()
'Sub procedure to give a day of the week message and today's date.
Dim dayNum As Integer
Dim theDate As Date
theDate = Date
dayNum = Weekday(Date)
Select Case dayNum
    Case 2: MsgBox "Today is Monday" & theDate
    Case 3: MsgBox "Today is Tuesday" & theDate
    Case 4: MsgBox "Today is Wednesday" & theDate
    Case 5: MsgBox "Today is Thursday" & theDate
    Case 6: MsgBox "Today is Friday" & theDate
    Case Else: MsgBox "Happy Weekend" & theDate
End Select
End Sub
```

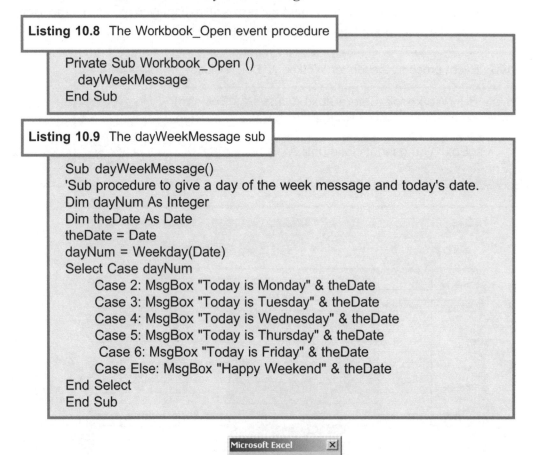

Figure 10.12 Screenshot of Listing 10.8 and 10.9

Creating context-sensitive Help

In Chapter 3, we looked at VBA built-in Help facilities. However, most users of Excel – or of any other Office application – will have had some experience with the Office Assistant. When clicked, this will deliver Help known as *Balloon Help* – so-called because of the way in which it is displayed (Figure 10.13). It is possible to customise the Help delivered by the balloon object, so that we can create context-sensitive Help, which could be of significant benefit to a user who needs support with some Excel application. This is one of several objects that Microsoft makes available to each of its Office applications. The Assistant displays inside the balloon a heading followed by a list of menu options and some buttons at the bottom.

The illustration shows the standard Excel/VBA Help, but you can customise this to application specific Help. For example, suppose it was necessary to include balloon Help to the user of the SALESMAN workbook. It could be invoked by using a macro button called *Help*. This button could be linked to a macro called *Assist*. We can see from Figure 10.14 that a balloon can contain a plethora of items – such as headings, buttons and text. They can also contain check boxes, radio buttons, and so on.

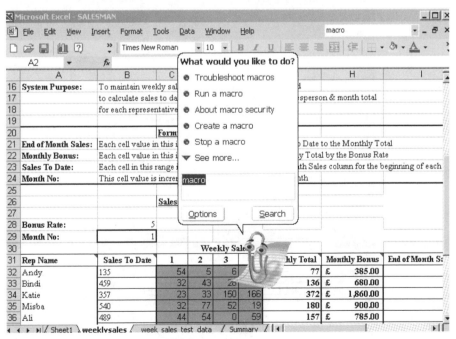

Figure 10.13 The Office Assistant delivering balloon Help

Worked example

This example creates context-sensitive balloon Help for supporting the use of the SALESMAN workbook. In this example, the user will be presented with a balloon whose title is: 'Help Choices for using the Salesman system'.

The first thing to do is to define a variable that can store a Balloon object. We can use a statement of the form:

```
Dim  myBalloon As Balloon
```

You can create a Balloon object by using a property called *NewBalloon*. and this is assigned to the balloon variable. When assigning any object variable, we can use a statement of the form:

```
Set myBalloon = Assistant.NewBalloon
```

Listing 10.10 contains the VBA code that will implement the customised help menu as displayed in Figure 10.14. Notice that a variable of type Balloon has been declared with the line:

```
Dim BlnLabels As Balloon
```

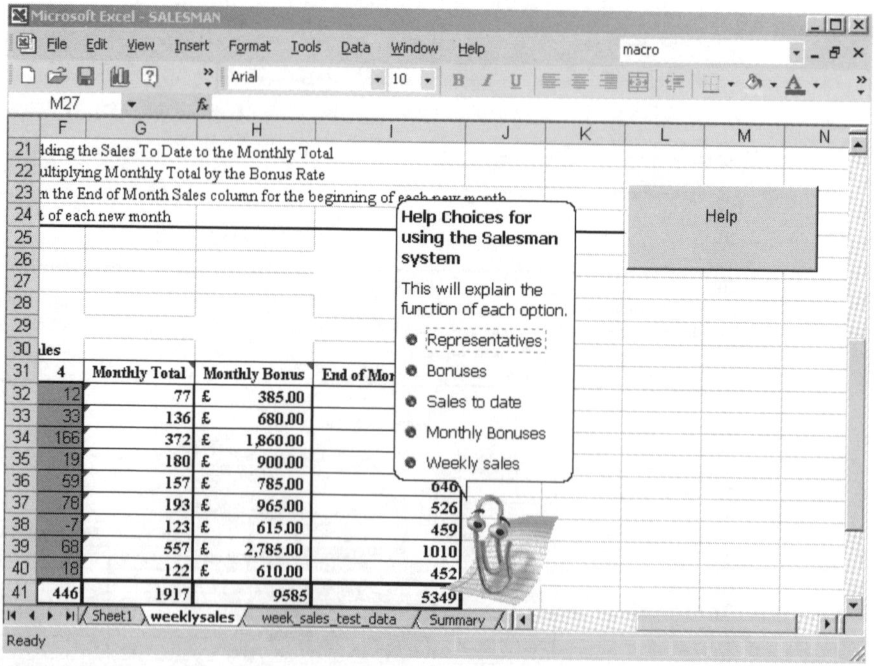

Figure 10.14 Further explanation of selected options using MsgBox

Also, a variable has been created called *IntReturnValue* whose purpose is to store the return value of the user's selected choice, in order to generate the appropriate explanation that follows the original selection. This variable has been defined as:

```
Dim IntReturnValue As Variant
```

Next, the balloon variable *BlnLabels* is assigned to a balloon object with the statement:

```
Set BlnLabels = Assistant.NewBalloon
```

The statement **Assistant.Visible** = **True** will make the balloon visible. The statement **With blnlabels** will then be used to assign each of the label choices as shown below:

```
With blnlabels
    .Heading = "Help Choices for using the Salesman system"
    .Text = "This will explain the function of each option."
    .Labels (1).Text = "Representatives"
    .Labels (2).Text = "Bonuses"
    .Labels (3).Text = "Sales to date"
    .Labels (4).Text = "Monthly Bonuses"
    .Labels (5).Text = "Weekly sales"
    .Button = msoBalloonTypeButtons
    .Show
End With
```

The heading is assigned using the *Heading* property of the balloon object:

```
.Heading = "Help Choices for using the Salesman system"
```

An optional supporting text statement is then used using the *Text* property of the balloon object:

```
.Text = "This will explain the function of each option."
```

The label choices can each be set using the *Labels* property as follows:

```
.Labels (1).Text = "Representatives"
```

When the choices are complete, the *Button* property as in the statement…

```
.Button = msoButtonSetNone
```

…specifies which buttons should appear at the bottom of the balloon when all the text choices have been completed. In this example, we have set this property to *None* so that no button will be displayed at the bottom of the balloon. The default value for this property is an **OK** button. Some other possible values for Button properties are listed in Table 10.1. The method **Show** is then used to display the balloon using the statement:

```
.Show
```

The next section of the program assigns the value (in the range 1 to 5) of the choice selected by using the statement:

```
IntReturnValue = blnlabels.Show
```

The statement:

```
Select Case IntReturnValue
```

Will then use the Select Case construct (see Chapter 6) to display a more detailed explanation when a choice is selected from the balloon. The full program listing is shown in Listing 10.10.

Listing 10.10 Code for customising balloon Help

```
Sub Assist()
  ActiveSheet.Unprotect
  Dim BlnLabels As Balloon
  Dim IntReturnValue As Variant
  Set BlnLabels = Assistant.NewBalloon
  Assistant.Visible = True
  With blnlabels
    .Heading = "Help Choices for using the Salesman system"
    .Text = "This will explain the function of each option."
    .Labels (1).Text = "Representatives"
    .Labels (2).Text = "Bonus Rate"
    .Labels (3).Text = "Sales to date"
    .Labels (4).Text = "Monthly Bonuses"
    .Labels (5).Text = "Weekly sales"
    .Button = msoButtonSetNone
    .Show
  End With
  IntReturnValue = blnlabels.Show
  Select Case IntReturnValue
    Case 1
      MsgBox "The representatives column displays each rep name
currently in the worksheet. This is the left-hand column and the rep names
are not sorted in any particular order"
    Case 2
      MsgBox "The Bonus rate is fixed for all representatives. The  bonus
rate can be read from cell B43"
    Case 3
      MsgBox "The sales to date column displays the total sales to date
for each representative during the current financial year."
    Case 4
      MsgBox "The monthly bonus column displays the total monthly
bonus accrued for each sales representative for the current month."
    Case 5
      MsgBox "The range weekly sales contains the cell grid running from
C32:F40 and displays each of the four weeks during the month."
  End Select
  ActiveSheet.Protect
End Sub
```

207

Table10.1 Some common properties of the Balloon object

Property	Purpose and Illustration of use
Heading	Used to display the heading text that appears in the balloon. .Heading = "Help Choices for using the Salesman system"
Text	Used to display text after the heading but before any labels, or check boxes .Text = "This will explain the function of each option."
Labels (index)	Used to create a BalloonLabel object. Index is an integer between 1 and 5. i.e., 5 choices are possible. .Labels (1).Text = "Representatives"
Button	Used to control the buttons at the bottom – possible values are: msoButtonSetOK – will display OK button only msoButtonSetNone – will display no buttons msoButtonSetYesNo – will display two buttons, labelled Yes and No msoButtonSetOKCancel – will display two buttons, OK and Cancel .Button = msoButtonSetNone
BalloonType	Used to format the labels that appear in the balloons. This property can be assigned to any of the following three values: . msoBalloonTypeButtons – will display the labels in button format .BalloonType = msoBalloonTypeButtons msoBalloonTypeBullets – will display the labels using bullet point format .BalloonType = msoBalloonTypeBullets msoBalloonTypeNumbers – will display the labels in number point format .BalloonType = msoBalloonTypeNumbers

Table10.2 Some common properties of the Assistant object

Property	Purpose and Illustration of use
NewBalloon	Creates a customised balloon for the Assistant. For example, Set BalloonObj = Assistant.NewBalloon
On	This is a Boolean property. Setting the value to True turns the property on. Setting the value to False turns the Assistant feature off. For example, Assistant. On=False will remove the Assistant
Visible	This again is a Boolean valued property.

Designing for the end user

An Excel/VBA application can be anything from a small task that performs a useful service to a large application that completely shields the user from Excel's basic interface perhaps using a combination of forms and automatic macros. Excel and VBA provide many features for developers to build applications that cater for different types of end users. The VBA programmer will need to consider who will use the applications and what sort of skills and experience they have. For example, a novice user – such as a data entry clerk – may find dialog boxes more helpful than a raw worksheet. This type of system could well be designed in a foolproof manner. On the other hand, managers may find an interface that automates the presentation of data – such as by using charts and graphs – more suitable. Thus, when designing an appropriate interface with an Excel /VBA application, the following points should be considered:

♦ What sort of interface should the application provide? Will it be appropriate for the end-users? This could turn out to be more complex than it first appears because users are unlikely to be a simple homogenous group. For example, some may have very basic knowledge and others may be expert Excel users. Perhaps some sort of adaptable interface may be appropriate in this situation.

♦ When a deliverable system contains macros, or user-defined functions, how will end users know that they exist? How will they find out how to use the macros? Will the system support these questions with Help, tutorials or training on how to use the macros provided by the application.

♦ When a system contains macros how will they run them? Will they:

a) Use **Tools** > **Macro** > **Macros...** from Excel and then select it by name?

b) Use a button, or customised menu item?

c) Use some other method like a dialog box?

♦ Is it possible or necessary to provide error checking and validation to help eliminate mistakes? Is it possible, or desirable, to lock and protect areas that need to be kept safe on the worksheet?

♦ Will sufficient on-line context-sensitive Help be available. How will the end-user know where to find it? Will there be, for example, Help buttons visible on the worksheets or will messages be supplied by macros?

In essence, the designer's decision regarding the interface styles will could be one of those described below. (**Note**: A hybrid of two or more of these styles may be used in practice.)

♦ The standard Excel worksheet interface may be suitable for those who are familiar with Excel, supported perhaps with comments to guide the user. For example, Figure 10.15 illustrates how comments can add explanation to the meaning of a column of data in a spreadsheet. In the fragment shown of the *weeklysales* worksheet of the SALESMAN workbook, the comment elaborates on the meaning of the *sales_to_date* range. Clearly, the designer of this type of interface will not require much knowledge of VBA.

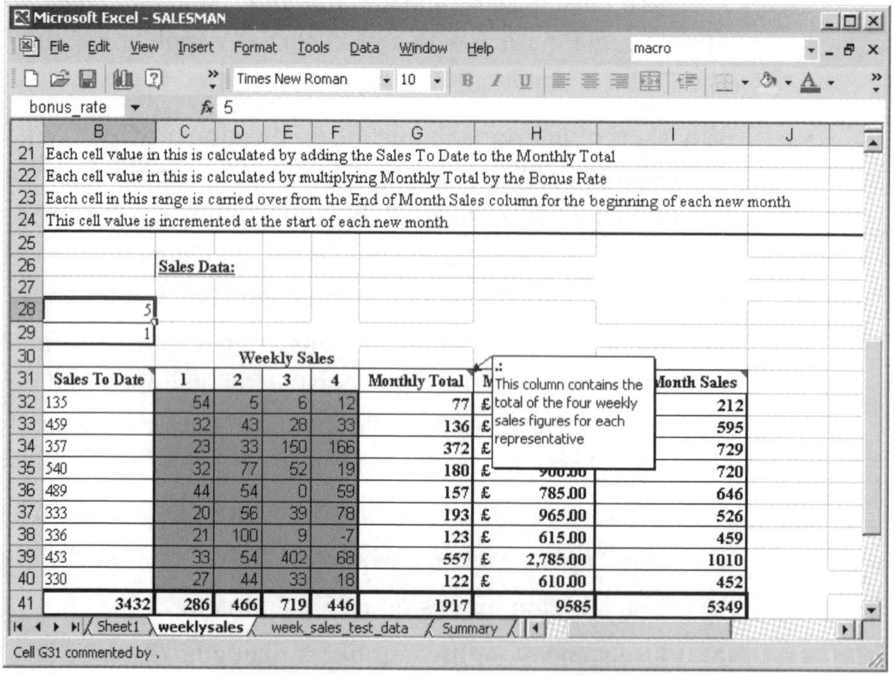

Figure 10.15 A raw worksheet interface supported by comments

♦ A user with an intermediate knowledge of Excel might benefit from the use of a formatted workbook. That is a workbook using worksheets that have locked or protected cell ranges, or perhaps use different fonts or colours to distinguish parts of the system, and so on. Figure 10.15 shows how the SALESMAN workbook has been formatted to enhance usability. Notice how the *Weekly Sales* range of the *weeklysales* worksheet has been coloured grey to make it stand out. Also, notice that the totals row at the foot of the data entry area is heavily bordered to make it stand out. An intermediate user may also benefit from the use of application specific balloon Help.

♦   A complete Excel novice user might be best served by designing customised dialog boxes for data entry, or forms with other window controls as a front end, possibly rendering the worksheet invisible to the user. For example, in Figure 10.16, a dialog box is used to input data for adding a new representative into worksheet cells. The design of this system was looked at earlier in this chapter. For a novice user with no knowledge of spreadsheets this interface style would be better than using a raw worksheet to add the data.

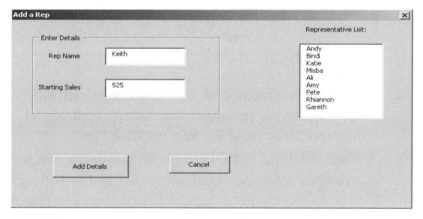

Figure 10.16 A data entry form suitable for a novice user

Exercises

1   Open a new workbook. Go to the VBE and insert a new form. Place on it three textboxes, with the labels FIRST, SECOND and RESULT, and three buttons labelled MAXIMUM, MINIMUM and QUIT – the layout should be similar to that in Figure 10.3. Write event handlers for the buttons. The form should accept two integers and show in the RESULT either the maximum or minimum, or quit the program, depending on the button clicked. Check your program by entering 6 in the FIRST and 15 in the SECOND textbox.

2   Open a new workbook. Write a **Workbook.SheetActivate** event procedure that will fill the cells A2, B2 and C2 with the values 1, 2 and 3 respectively whenever the user activates a worksheet. Test the results.

3   Study the following code and explain what you think it does:

```
Private Sub Workbook_NewSheet (ByVal Sh As Object)
    Range ("A1:A10").Value = "Month"
End Sub
```

4   Open a new workbook. Write a **Worksheet_Activate** event procedure that will display the message "You have entered Sheet3" whenever Sheet3 becomes the active sheet. Test the procedure.

5   Open the SALESMAN workbook and select the summary worksheet. Create the form shown in Figure 10.17 and write the event code that will enable a user to enter a rep name from the rep name list, and enter the highest and lowest sales in the boxes from the worksheet. If the user enters an invalid rep name, i.e., one that is not in the list, then the form should be unloaded. (**Hint**: You can use the procedure shown on page 137 to find the rep name from the list and then use the offset method to reference and transfer the highest and lowest sales to the form.)

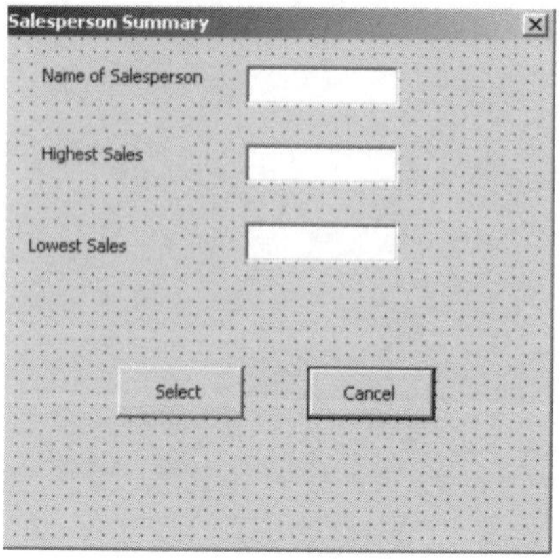

Figure 10.17

Appendices

ASCII codes 214

Events 215

   Worksheet events 215

   Workbook events 216

   Chart events 217

   Application events 218

Further reading 219

Useful VBA websites 220

ASCII codes

DEC	ASCII	DEC	ASCII	DEC	ASCII	DEC	ASCII
0	NULL	32	(SP)	64	@	96	‘
1	SOH	33	!	65	A	97	a
2	STX	34	"	66	B	98	b
3	ETX	35	#	67	C	99	c
4	EOT	36	$	68	D	100	d
5	ENQ	37	%	69	E	101	e
6	ACK	38	&	70	F	102	f
7	BEL	39	‘	71	G	103	g
8	BS	40	(	72	H	104	h
9	HT	41	)	73	I	105	i
10	LF	42	*	74	J	106	j
11	VT	43	+	75	K	107	k
12	FF	44	,	76	L	108	l
13	CR	45	-	77	M	109	m
14	SO	46	.	78	N	110	n
15	SI	47	/	79	O	111	o
16	DLE	48	0	80	P	112	p
17	DC1	49	1	81	Q	113	q
18	DC2	50	2	82	R	114	r
19	DC3	51	3	83	S	115	s
20	DC4	52	4	84	T	116	t
21	NAK	53	5	85	U	117	u
22	SYN	54	6	86	V	118	v
23	ETB	55	7	87	W	119	w
24	CAN	56	8	88	X	120	x
25	EM	57	9	89	Y	121	y
26	SUB	58	:	90	Z	122	z
27	ESC	59	;	91	[	123	{
28	FS	60	<	92	\	124		
29	GS	61	=	93	]	125	}
30	RS	62	>	94	^	126	~
31	US	63	?	95	_	127	(space)

Events

The following tables list some of the more useful events for the event procedures for the objects listed in Chapter 10.

Worksheet events

Event name	Description
Worksheet_Activate	Occurs when a worksheet is activated
Worksheet_BeforeDoubleClick	Occurs when the user double-clicks on a cell ✗
Worksheet_BeforeRightClick	Occurs when the user right-clicks on a cell ✗
Worksheet_Calculate	Occurs when a cell on the worksheet is calculated.
Worksheet_Change	Occurs when the value of a cell is changed, not following a change as the result of a calculation.
Worksheet_Deactivate	Occurs when a worksheet is deactivated, or another worksheet is displayed.
Worksheet_SelectionChange	Occurs when the selection is moved to a new range.

✗   *A Cancel parameter is provided with this event.*

Workbook events

Event name	Description
Workbook_Activate	Occurs when the workbook is activated.
Workbook_BeforeClose	Occurs when the workbook is closed. ✘
Workbook_BeforePrint	Occurs when the workbook is printed. ✘
Workbook_BeforeSave	Occurs when the workbook is saved. ✘
Workbook_Deactivate	Occurs when the workbook is deactivated, not when you switch applications.
Workbook_NewSheet	Occurs when a new worksheet is added to the workbook.
Workbook_Open	Occurs when the workbook is opened.
Workbook_SheetActivate	The workbook implementation of the Worksheet_Activate event.
Workbook_SheetBeforeDoubleClick	The workbook implementation of the Worksheet_BeforeDoubleClick event. ✘
Workbook_SheetBeforeRightClick	The workbook implementation of the Worksheet_BeforeRightClick event. ✘
Workbook_SheetCalculate	The workbook implementation of the Worksheet_Calculate event.
Workbook_SheetChange	The workbook implementation of the Worksheet_Change event.
Workbook_SheetDeactivate	The workbook implementation of the Worksheet_Deactivate event.
Workbook_SheetSelectionChange	The workbook implementation of the Worksheet_SelectionChange event.

✘   *A Cancel parameter is provided with this event.*

Chart events

Event name	Description
Chart_Activate	Occurs when the chart sheet is activated.
Chart_BeforeDoubleClick	Occurs when the user double-clicks on the chart sheet. ✗
Chart_BeforeRightClick	Occurs when the user right-clicks on the chart sheet. ✗
Chart_Calculate	Occurs when the chart is calculated or an element of the chart is changed.
Chart_Deactivate	Occurs when the chart sheet is deactivated.
Chart_MouseDown	Occurs when the user presses a mouse button while over the chart.
Chart_MouseMove	Occurs when the user moves the mouse over the chart.
Chart_MouseUp	Occurs when the user releases the mouse button.
Chart_Resize	Occurs when the chart is resized.
Chart_Select	Occurs when the user selects the chart.
Chart_SeriesChange	Occurs when the value of a data point is changed.

✗ A Cancel parameter is provided with this event.

Application events

Event name	Description
App_NewWorkbook	Occurs when a new workbook is added.
App_SheetActivate	The Application implementation of the Worksheet_Activate event.
App_SheetBeforeDoubleClick	The Application implementation of the Worksheet_BeforeDoubleClick event. ✘
App_SheetBeforeRightClick	The Application implementation of the Worksheet_BeforeRightClick event. ✘
App_SheetCalculate	The Application implementation of the Worksheet_Calculate event.
App_SheetChange	The Application implementation of the Worksheet_Change event.
App_SheetDeactivate	The Application implementation of the Worksheet_Deactivate event.
App_SheetSelectionChange	The Application implementation of the Worksheet_SelectionChange event.
App_WindowActivate	The Application implementation of the Workbook_WindowActivate event.
App_WindowDeactivate	The Application implementation of the Workbook_WindowDeactivate event.
App_WindowResize	The Application implementation of the Workbook_WindowResize event.
App_WorkbookActivate	The Application implementation of the Workbook_Activate event.
App_WorkbookBeforeClose	The Application implementation of the Workbook_BeforeClose event. ✘
App_WorkbookBeforePrint	The Application implementation of the Workbook_BeforePrint event. ✘
App_WorkbookBeforeSave	The Application implementation of the Workbook_BeforeSave event. ✘
App_WorkbookDeactivate	The Application implementation of the Workbook_Deactivate event.
App_WorkbookNewSheet	The Application implementation of the Workbook_NewSheet event.
App_WorkbookOpen	The Application implementation of the Workbook_Open event.

✘ *A Cancel parameter is provided with this event.*

Further reading

Deitel, H.M., Deitel, P.J, Nieto, T.R. (1999), *Visual Basic – 6 How to Program*, Prentice Hall.

Graham, Ian (1992), *Object-oriented methods*, Addison Wesley.

Green, J. (1999), *Excel 2000 VBA Programmer's Reference*, Wrox Press.

Lomax, P. (1998), *VB & VBA in a Nutshell*, O'Reilly.

Pressman. R. S. (1994), *Software Engineering – A Practitioner's Approach*, Mc Graw-Hill.

Roman, S. (1999), *Writing Excel Macros*, O'Reilly.

Zak, D. (2000), *Visual Basic for Applications*, Thomson Learning.

Useful VBA websites

http://support.microsoft.com/support/help/examples.asp

http://www.searchvb.com

http://www.vbexplorer.com

http://www.vbwm.com

http://www.vbtt.com

http://search.support.microsoft.com/kb/c.asp

http://www.j-walk.com/ss/excel/eee/index.htm

Index

Symbols

8086 chip 8

A

Add Watch... 154
And 122
Apple II microcomputer 7
Apple Macintosh 8
Application events 218
Application object methods 88
Application software 9
Arrays 107
   dynamic 108
   index 107
Artificial intelligence languages 16
Assembler languages 14
ASCII codes 214
Assistant object, properties 208
Auto_Close 57
Auto_Open 57

B

Balloon Help 203
Balloon object 204
   properties 208
Basic 18
BBC Micro 7
BITs 14
Black box testing 151
ByRef 182
ByVal 182

C

Calculations 61
Case Else 124
Chart events 217
Click() event 196
Comments 47
Comparison operators 114
Compiler 14
Computers, brief history 4
Constants 104
CP/M 10

D

Data entry forms 193
Data types 93
   comparison of 116
   user-defined 105
Debug toolbar 154
Debug.Print 160
Debugging 148
DEC PDP minicomputers 6
Dim 108
DisplayAlerts 88
Do ... Loop 139
Do ...Loop While 140
Do Until... Loop 139
Do While ...Loop 139
Do...Loop Until 140
DOS 10

E

Editor window 46

End user, designing for 209
ENIAC computer 4
Event procedures 199
Events 70, 215
Excel, origins 19
Excel charts, macros for 36
Excel objects 75
Exit For 137
Explicit declarations 97

F

For Each ... Next 80, 130
For... Next 132
Forms 188
   designing 194
   event handlers 195
   Toolbox 189
Functions 172
   calling 175
   defining 174
   using parameters 179

G

GUI (graphic user interface) 11

H

Hardware 3
Harvard Mark 1 5
Help 63
   context-sensitive 203
High-level languages 13

I

IBM 701 EPDM 5
IBM PC 8
If statements 116
If...ElseIf... 120
If...Then 116
If...Then...Else 118
Immediate window 160
Initialize() procedure 195
InputBox 52
InputBox method, in Application object 88
Integrated development environment (IDE) 15
Intel 8
Interpreter 14

K

Keyboard shortcuts 29

L

Leo 5
Line break, debugging 149
Line breaks, in MsgBox 56
Linux 9
Logical errors 150
Logical operators 122
Loop structures, which to use 144
Loop termination 143
Low-level languages 13

M

Macros
   and buttons 33

assigning to a toolbar 34
cell references 31
defined 24
recording 27
testing 151
tips for running 59
Maintenance 166
Methods 69
Modules 48
  creating 65
Moore's Law 4
MsgBox 53
  buttons 54

N

Named ranges 84
Not 122

O

Object Browser 77
Object collections 71
Object-oriented programming (OOP) 16, 68
Objects, referencing 70
Offset method 87
On Error GoTo 161
OnEntry 57
OnSheetActivate 57
Operating system 9
Operators 114
  summary 127
Option explicit 97
Or 122

P

Parameters
  and arguments 174
  passing 182
Procedures, defined 49
Programming errors 148
Programming languages 13
Project Explorer 45
Properties pane 46
Pseudocode 50

R

Range object 84
Run-time errors 149

S

ScreenUpdating 88
Security levels 40
Select case 123
Set keyword 100
Step Into 157
Step Out 158
Step Over 157
String comparisons 115
Structured English 50
Subs 170
Syntax errors 148

T

Testing 151
Third-generation languages (3GL) 14
Toggle Breakpoint 156

Trapping errors 161
Type 105

U

User-defined data types 105

V

Validating data 80
Variables 92
    assigning values 99
    declaration 96
    names 95
    types 93
VBA Editor 46
VBA environment 45

VBA modules 57
Visual Basic
    origins 18
    toolbar 39
Visual Basic for Applications 20
Visual programming 15

W

Watch window 154
What-if questions 26
Windows 11
With...End With 76
Workbook events 216
Worksheet events 215